TOP 10
SICILY

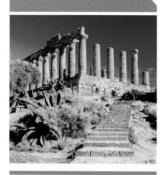

Top 10 Sicily Highlights

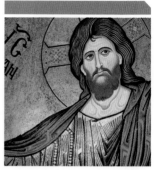

The Top 10 of Everything

CONTENTS

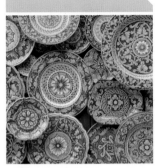

Sicily Area by Area

Streetsmart

Within each Top 10 list in this book, no hierarchy of quality or popularity is implied. All 10 are, in the editor's opinion, of roughly equal merit.

Title page, front cover and spine Port city of Catania, Sicily, with Mount Etna in the distance **Back cover, clockwise fom top left** *The historic city of Syracuse on the Ionian coast of Sicily; view from Taormina at sunset; Mount Etna; Catania; the picturesque town of Forza d'Agrò, Messina*

The rapid rate at which the world is changing is constantly keeping the DK Eyewitness team on our toes. While we've worked hard to ensure that this edition of Sicily is accurate and up-to-date, we know that opening hours alter, standards shift, prices fluctuate, places close and new ones pop up in their stead. So, if you notice we've got something wrong or left something out, we want to hear about it. Please get in touch at **travelguides@dk.com**

Welcome to
Sicily

Sicily has always been an intriguing crossroads of cultures and civilizations. Located at the tip of the Italian peninsula, its strategic position in the Mediterranean sea attracted visitors and invaders alike. Nowadays, the wealth of ancient sights, stunning natural beauty and family-friendly beaches make Sicily an ideal and unforgettable holiday destination. With DK Eyewitness Top 10 Sicily, it's yours to explore.

Over the centuries Sicily has been part of Greater Greece, a Roman province, a Byzantine stronghold, an Arab Caliphate, a Norman kingdom, a pawn for Spain and the Bourbons, and ultimately part of a unified Italy. The vestiges of bygone eras are ever-present, so it is no surprise that the island has developed a powerful identity all of its own – so much so that the great German writer Johann Wolfgang von Goethe said that "without Sicily, Italy creates no image in the soul; here is the key to everything".

Today, Sicily still holds that key: the largest island in the Mediterranean is an explosion of colours and idiosyncrasies that are both enticing and baffling to visitors. But as you stroll past the crumbling ruins, experience the liveliness of the markets as locals go about their everyday business, observe friends playing cards in the town square, and feast on the delectable food the island is renowned for, it is impossible not to be charmed.

Whether you're visiting for a weekend or a week, our Top 10 guide brings together the best of everything Sicily has to offer, from sunny beaches and verdant mountains to archaeological treasures and ornate royal palaces. The guide has useful tips throughout, from seeking out what's free to places off the beaten track, plus seven easy-to-follow itineraries designed to tie together a clutch of sights in a short space of time. Add inspiring photography and detailed maps, and you've got the essential pocket-sized travel companion. **Enjoy the book, and enjoy Sicily**.

Clockwise from top: **Cefalù**, **La Scala dei Turchi**, **church of San Cataldo in Palermo**, **Favignana**, **Ten Girls in Bikinis mosaic at Villa Romana del Casale**, **Stromboli**, **Temple E at Selinunte**

Exploring Sicily

Given its size and number of sites, it's impossible to see all of Sicily in less than a week. Here we help you maximise your time, with a seven-day itinerary covering the key sights in Sicily, and a two-day itinerary just for the Aeolian Islands.

Seven Days in Sicily

Day ❶

Spend the morning visiting old **Palermo** (see pp12–13) – don't miss the **Palazzo dei Normanni** and the **Cappella Palatina**. Lunch at one of the city's outdoor markets. Take bus 389 from Piazza Indipendenza to the bottom of the town, then walk to **Monreale** (see pp14–15), a glorious church from the Norman era. Marvel at the glittering 12th-century mosaics inside, then explore the adjacent cloisters.

Villa Romana del Casale

Day ❷

Hire a car or take the train to **Segesta** (see p44), the romantic site of the only freestanding limestone temple in Sicily, as well as a 3rd-century BC theatre with stunning views. Head to **Erice** (see p99) and visit the Castle of Venus, then head to Maria Grammatico to buy sweets. Stay the night at Agriturismo Antica Tenuta dei Pignatelli in **Castelvetrano**, "City of Olives and Temples" (see p102).

Day ❸

Drive or take the bus to **Selinunte** (see pp36–9) and see what remains of the mighty Selinus Acropolis. The Valle dei Templi in **Agrigento** (see pp32–5) is home to beautiful temples. The Temple of Concord features a Paleochristian church.

Day ❹

Drive to **Villa Romana del Casale** near Piazza Armerina (see pp30–31). View Roman-era mosaics, including the famous Ten Girls in Bikinis. Drive to **Noto** (see pp28–9) and spend the afternoon exploring this Baroque town. Stay in **Syracuse** (see pp24–7) at the Grand Hotel Minareto (see p144).

The Temple of Concordia, Agrigento, dates from 430 BC but is remarkably intact.

Key
— Two-day Itinerary
— Seven-day Itinerary

The Aeolian Islands each have their own unique character and beauty.

way to the beautiful Teatro Antico. Make sure you take part in the traditional *passeggiata* (evening stroll). Before leaving Sicily, visit the beaches at lovely **Giardini Naxos** *(see p109)*, just below Taormina, where Greek colonization began.

Two Days on the Aeolian Islands

Day ❶
MORNING
From **Milazzo** go to the Aeolian Islands *(see pp16–17)*. Disembark at **Lipari** for the Museo Archeologico Regionale Eoliano *(see p51)*.
AFTERNOON
Travel to the eastern isles with Avventurisole Viaggi Eolie *(www. eolietour.com)*. Pause on **Panarea**, sample pizza on **Stromboli**, and watch the volcano from the boat.

Day ❷
MORNING
Island hopping starts from **Alicudi**. Take the hydrofoil and head eastwards to **Filicudi**, famous for its lentils and capers. Next it's east to Salina, where Malvasia grapes are harvested.
AFTERNOON
Back on Lipari, visit the stunning Cava del Pomice, a former pumice rock quarry, now a beach. Finish the day with a drink at Il Piccolo Bar on Via Marina Garibaldi, Canneto.

Day ❺
Syracuse was once the most powerful city of the Mediterranean – its Greek Theatre held 20,000 people. Don't miss the Ear of Dionysius in the Latomia del Paradiso and the Temple of Apollo. Explore the beautiful island of Ortygia. Take in the Piazza Duomo, then visit the Cathedral, built within the Temple of Minerva. Finish at Castello Maniace.

Day ❻
Visit **Mount Etna** *(see pp20–21)* from Piano Provenzana. Take the cable car at Rifugio Sapienza, and once you've arrived at base camp, hop into one of the jeeps that shuttle visitors to the top. Take in the Valle del Bove, a valley filled with lava flow. Stop in at a beekeeper's and buy some honey.

Day ❼
Taormina *(see pp18–19)* is home to Italy's glitterati. Visit Palazzo Corvaja and the Odeon, before making your

Top 10 Sicily Highlights

Temple of Juno, Valley of
the Temples, Agrigento

TOP 10 Sicily Highlights

The island of Sicily is Italy's largest region and its most varied. There are offshore islands, cliffs and beaches, rugged mountains, rolling wheatfields and volcanoes. Sicily's history is also of note. The Greeks, Romans, Byzantines and Normans all left their mark on the island.

Palermo ①

The island capital's history is best seen in its architecture – medieval quarters with crumbling Baroque churches, exquisite Arab-Norman churches and precious Art Nouveau *palazzi* (see pp12–13).

② Monreale

A spectacular Norman monument, the mosaic cycle at Monreale Cathedral is a wonder of the medieval world (see pp14–15).

San Vito lo Capo
Trapani
Egadi Islands
Segesta
Marsala
Val di Mázara
Chiusa Sclafani
Selinunte ⑩
Sciacca
① Palermo
② Monreale
San Cipirello
Corleone
Cerda
Alia
Caltabellotta
Eraclea Minoa
Agrigento ⑨

③ Aeolian Islands

These seven volcanic islands offer a live volcano, black lava beaches, and food and wines flavoured by the sun (see pp16–17).

④ Taormina

Sicily's first resort has welcomed visitors for centuries. The town offers breathtaking views, an ancient theatre, and cafés and terraces overlooking the sea (see pp18–19).

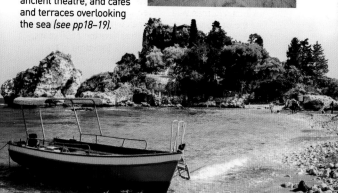

5 Mount Etna

This, the largest and most active volcano in Europe, looms powerfully over eastern Sicily (see pp20–21).

6 Syracuse

This once mighty Greek colony and rival to Athens is today a thriving modern city. Traces of its former glory include a Baroque cathedral and a Greek theatre (see pp24–7).

7 Noto

Destroyed by an earthquake in 1693, Noto was rebuilt during the 1700s, when the Baroque style was at its height (see pp28–9).

8 Villa Romana del Casale

The extensive mosaic decorations of this luxurious Roman villa are the best preserved of their kind in the world (see pp30–31).

9 Agrigento

The famed Valle dei Templi is home to ruined Greek temples that stand, as they have for 2,500 years, against a backdrop of the distant sea (see pp32–5).

10 Selinunte

Another of Sicily's remarkable ancient sites, the romantic remains of Greek Selinus reign spectacularly from a promontory high above the sea. This is the largest archaeological park in Europe (see pp36–9).

🔟⭐ Palermo

When the Phoenicians founded Palermo in 735 BC, they named it Zyz ("flower"), such was the beauty of its verdant hills, dotted with fruit trees and native flora. This greenery is still visible, especially along the paths that wind their way up to the former Phoenician fortress, now the Palazzo dei Normanni. Palermo is now Sicily's buzzing artistic centre, home to grand opera houses, tiny theatres and avant-garde museums. There's plenty of culture, whether you're visiting the former church of San Giovanni degli Eremiti or meandering past the delightfully stuccoed Oratorio di San Lorenzo.

Cathedral ①
Founded in 1185, the cathedral **(right)** is an eclectic mix of architectural styles. Admire the 12-century apse, the porphyry royal tombs, the crypt and the treasury housing Empress Constance's crown.

San Cataldo ②
This church **(above)** is an example of the Arab-Norman architecture that flourished across Sicily under Norman control. Its roof has three domes and Arab-style parapets.

Oratorio di San Lorenzo ③
With a white stucco interior by the sculptor Giacomo Serpotta, the 16th-century oratory housed a Caravaggio painting, until it was stolen in 1969.

Palermo

500 metres
(547 yards)

400 metres
(437 yards)

Palazzo dei Normanni ④
The royal palace is testament to the city's Arab-Norman heritage. Its Punic foundations, the dazzling mosaics of La Stanza di Ruggero and the Torre Gioaria (Arab wind tower) embody its long history.

Palazzo Steri ⑤
Grafitti on the walls serves as a poignant reminder that this was the seat of the Inquisition in the 17th century.

7 Cappella Palatina

Commissioned in 1129 by Roger II, the chapel **(left)** in the Palazzo dei Normanni harmoniously combines western and Arab styles. The Arab ceiling is painted with animals and greenery. It also shows a Christ Pantocrator, produced by Byzantine masters using gold and silver tesserae, offering his blessing from the cupola and the apse.

8 La Zisa

This castle, built in the 12th century by Arab masons, is inspired by Moorish architecture. Its name comes from *al-Azīz*, meaning "splendid".

9 San Giovanni degli Eremiti

Founded in 1132, and set amid lush gardens, San Giovanni **(above)** was the richest monastery in Sicily. Five red domes, typical of Arab style, mark the exterior, while the interior of the church has only remnants of its original decoration.

6 La Martorana

Santa Maria dell' Ammiraglio **(below)** is called La Martorana after 12th-century nun Eloisa Martorana, who used to decorate the church *(see p91)* with mosaics.

THE NORMANS IN SICILY

In 1061 Norman soldier Roger de Hauteville took advantage of internal Arab conflict in order to invade the island with a small group of crusaders. He was the first of five powerful Norman kings who, over the next century, turned Sicily into a wealthy monarchy. By 1266, they left behind an island endowed with splendid buildings and culture that blended western and Arab influences.

NEED TO KNOW

Cathedral: **MAP K5**; Via Vittorio Emanuele; open 7am–7pm Mon–Sat, 8am–7pm Sun & hols (Monumental area: 9am–6pm Mon–Sat; 10am–6pm Sun & hols); adm €12 for the crypt, treasury and royal tombs

Palazzo dei Normanni: **MAP J6**; Piazza Indipendenza; open 9:30am–4:30pm Mon–Sat (to 12:30pm Sun & hols), royal apartments: closed Tue–Thu; adm €19 Fri–Mon & hols, €15.50 Tue–Thu

Cappella Palatina: **MAP J6**; open 8:30am–2:30pm Mon–Thu (to 4:30pm Fri & Sat, 12:30pm Sun & hols); adm (combined with Palazzo dei Normanni)

10 Palazzo della Cuba

Constructed in 1180 for William II of Sicily as his personal recreation pavilion, Palazzo della Cuba was designed by the Arab artists who were still living in the city after the Norman conquest.

TOP 10 ★ Monreale

The cathedral at Monreale, high above the fertile Conca d'Oro (Golden Shell), overlooks Palermo. King William II founded the majestic cathedral and Benedictine monastery in 1174, and a medieval village soon grew up around them. Despite its rather austere exterior, inside the cathedral has spectacular decoration, which constitutes the most extensive and important mosaic cycle of its kind in Sicily. The entrance is in Piazza Vittorio Emanuele.

1 Apse Exterior

In contrast to the rest of the exterior, which is relatively plain, the triple apse (below) is decorated with intricate stonework that forms interlacing arches of limestone and lava.

KING WILLIAM II

William II's political rival Walter of the Mill, the Archbishop of Palermo, and his faction of clerics and landowners had become too powerful. By building a cathedral at Monreale (specifically a Benedictine abbey and thus independent of the archbishop), King William was able to redistribute the balance of power. The beautiful cathedral, with dazzling mosaic decoration, was completed in 1189.

2 Façade

The façade, with a bronze door, is bracketed by two asymmetrical square towers and bears decorative stonework. The front porch is an 18th-century addition.

4 Cloister

The calm cloister (above) combines Arab-styled arches, carved capitals decorated with mosaic patterns, and a 12th-century fountain in the geometric garden.

3 Interior

The interior (below) has granite columns with Roman Corinthian capitals supporting around 6,500 sq m (70,000 sq ft) of brilliant mosaics.

5 Side Apse Mosaics

Above the thrones to either side of the main apse are portraits depicting the coronation of William II by Christ himself, and presenting the cathedral to the Madonna, a scene blessed by the hand of God.

8 Nave Mosaics

These Old and New Testament scenes were educational panels for the illiterate parishioners of the time. They include the Creation, the Sacrifice of Isaac (above) and Noah's Ark.

9 Apse Mosaic of Christ

The enormous image of the Christ Pantocrator embraces his followers with curved arms and outstretched hands from up high.

10 North Transept

Here visitors can walk on spectacular Cosmati mosaics arranged in intricate patterns, such as the four hares in a circle. Head into the Capella Roano to see some exquisite Baroque craftsmanship.

Monreale

6 Mosaics of Martyr Saints

One of the martyr saints shown is St Thomas à Becket, canonized the year before the church was founded. It is his earliest known portrait.

7 Ceilings

The choir ceiling has guilded motifs and decorative patterns. The nave ceiling was restored after a fire in 1811.

NEED TO KNOW

MAP C2 ■ Piazza Guglielmo II 1, Monreale ■ AST buses: from Palermo (Piazza Indipendenza) to Monreale ■ www. duomomonreale.com

Cathedral: open 9am–1pm & 2–5:15pm Mon–Sat; 2–5:15pm Sun; adm €4

Cloister: 091 6404403; open 9am–7pm Mon–Sat;

(to 1:30pm Sun) & hols; adm €6

■ Have a coffee or *gelato* at the Bar Baby O' in Piazza Guglielmo before or after your visit.

■ The church is popular for weddings – if one is in progress when you visit, go to the cloisters and gardens first.

TOP 10 ⭐ Aeolian Islands

This chain of volcanic islands offers a small-town atmosphere, flavourful cuisine, history and natural beauty. Each of the islands has its own character: Lipari is bright white with pumice; the fertile volcanic soil of Salina grows verdant grapevines and forests with rock formations like mounds of whipped cream; on Vulcano cooled molten lava has left cliffs like rows of elephants' legs. Beaches are powdery grey-white with pumice or black with powdered lava, and the sea is clean, clear and full of marine life.

1 Pollara Beach, Salina

The beach at Pollara **(above)** has large pebbles as well as patches of sand. The water is great for snorkelling, with sea urchins, octopuses and other sea life.

2 Perciato di Pollara, Salina

This stone arch **(below)** swoops down from the cliff and comes to rest in the sea, creating a natural rock bridge. Visitors can get to the breathtaking Perciato via land or sea and then swim around the rocks.

3 Stromboli

A storied Aeolian volcano, Stromboli has been active for over two millennia, spewing sparks and red-hot rocks into the air, although you can only see them at night. Excursions are popular and available from the other islands.

NEED TO KNOW

MAP F1

Museo Archeologico Regionale Eoliano: Via del Castello, Lipari; 090 9880174; open 9am–6:30pm daily (to 1pm on public hols; winter by appt only); adm €6

■ It is best to stick to small, unassuming *trattorie* for good food at better prices.

■ The island chain is made up of fragile volcanic stone, so watch out for falling rocks (*caduta massi*).

7 Museo Archeologico Regionale Eoliano

The museum features items from the islands' Neolithic settlements, as well as impressive Greek and Roman displays **(left)**.

4 Sulphur Emissions, Vulcano

Sulphur emissions still seep from the main crater on Vulcano, and all over the island the vapour rises out of the craggy ground. The earth is a bright yellow **(below)** and there are many *fanghi* (mudbaths).

OBSIDIAN AND PUMICE

The volcanic by-products obsidian and pumice have played important roles in Lipari's commerce. The heavy, dense, glass-like black obsidian was crafted into knives and arrowheads in the Neolithic period and was valued and widely traded.
The quarrying of white, porous pumice was the major industry at Lipari, where the enormous quarries ground the rock for use in a variety of industries worldwide.

9 Alicudi and Filicudi

Tiny Alicudi **(below)** and Filicudi are the furthest-west and least-developed islands of the archipelago. They are perhaps the prettiest of the islands, with a sparse population, few cars and white-washed houses with breezy terraces.

5 Panarea

The tiniest island of the Aeolian archipelago is also its most exclusive. Panarea is known for its coves, clear water, rocky islets and nightlife. It also has a Bronze Age settlement.

6 Pumice Mines, Lipari

Lipari's biggest industry used to be pumice mining, until UNESCO urged the government to stop this industrial exploitation. Pumice is still so plentiful you'll find pieces of it washing up onto beaches, bobbing in the water and being sold in shops.

8 Marina Corta, Lipari

Smaller craft dock here, under this castle rock. In summer it bustles with activity; in winter you will see only the odd fisherman mending his nets.

10 Malvasia delle Lipari

This is the famed wine of the islands. White grapes are cultivated, harvested late and left to shrivel on cane mats before fermentation.

🔟⭐ Taormina

On Monte Tauro, with views of the rocky coastline, the blue-green sea and breathtaking Mount Etna, Taormina was founded in 304 BC as a colony of powerful Syracuse. The town endured a typical Sicilian history, falling first to the Romans, then to the Arabs, Normans and Spanish. During the 1800s Taormina became a stop on the Grand Tour and has been host to foreign visitors ever since. With its plethora of restaurants, hotels and shops, beaches and gardens, it is Sicily's most popular holiday destination.

① Santuario Madonna della Rocca

Affording heavenly views, this 17th-century church was built where a shepherd sheltering from a storm claimed to see the Virgin Mary.

③ Teatro Antico

With a spectacular view as a backdrop, the Greeks built this theatre **(right)** in the 3rd century BC, but what can be seen today was refurbished by the Romans in the 1st century AD.

② Mazzarò

Below Taormina are a few lovely beaches, such as Mazzarò **(above)**. Tiny Isola Bella nearby is linked to the coast by a strip of sand.

④ Piazza Vittorio Emanuele

The Palazzo Corvaja, is an architectural mix of Arab, Norman and Catalan Gothic elements. The Baroque Santa Caterina church is backed by the ruins of a Roman Odeon that is free to visit.

⑤ Piazza del Duomo

The Baroque fountain in the piazza bears a centaur, the symbol of Taormina, here atypically female. The 13th-century Chiesa Madre is dedicated to San Nicolò.

NEED TO KNOW

MAP H3

Teatro Antico: Via Teatro Greco 12; 094 223220; open 9am–1 hour before sunset daily; adm €10

■ After visiting the Teatro Antico, stop at the Wunderbar Café *(Piazza IX Aprile 7)* for a drink and some people-watching.

Taormina

8 Villa Comunale Gardens

With great views down to Giardini Naxos *(see p109)*, these well-tended gardens **(left)** have palm and banana trees, birds of paradise, exotic plants, many whimsical buildings and a monument to Taormina's sailors.

D H LAWRENCE IN TAORMINA

A storied hideaway of Greek kings, Taormina was a popular stop for many famous visitors on the so-called Grand Tour of Europe. For two years in the early 1920s, novelist D H Lawrence and his wife Frieda lived in the seaside town. It is believed that it was here that he wrote his titular novel, *Lady Chatterley's Lover,* inspired by the musings of an English woman he had met during his sojourn.

10 Corso Umberto I

Locals make their *passeggiata* (nightly stroll) on the Corso **(above)**, starting at Porta Messina, crossing lively piazzas with *gelaterie*, bars, shops and crowds to end at Porta Catania.

6 Piazza IX Aprile

This is a lovely square, where you are spoiled for choice between the sea views and people-watching at the many outdoor cafés. The Wunderbar plays live music in the evenings.

9 Borgo Medievale

The clock tower **(below)** is the gateway to the medieval part of town. The Corso is narrower here, and while the shops are the usual mix of clothing and souvenirs, the shop fronts have kept their medieval character.

7 Castelmola Walk

Take the Via Crucis path to the summit of Monte Tauro from Via Circonvallazione to enjoy the spectacular views and the ruins of the medieval castle.

TOP 10 ⭐ Mount Etna

Mount Etna, Europe's largest volcano, with many craters and a height of 3,330 m (10,925 ft), is one of the most active in the world. The Greeks knew it as home to Hephaestus, god of fire, whereas for the Arabs, it was Mongibello (Mountain of Mountains). Today, the Parco dell'Etna encompasses the volcano, where farmers produce wine, honey and fruit in the lava-rich soil. It offers hiking and, in season, skiing, as well as the occasional eruption of red sparks and lava. In 2013, it became a UNESCO World Heritage Site.

③ Visitor Centre
Visitors can find a trained guide at the Rifugio Sapienza Etna Sud (left). Walks start at the top cable-car station; they vary in length and can sometimes include a jeep transfer to see the lava flows.

DRAMATIC ERUPTIONS

Some of Etna's most devastating eruptions (see p112) were in 1381 and 1669, when the lava reached Catania. Since then, notable eruptions include one that wiped out Mascali in 1928 and another that killed nine tourists in 1979. Between 1991 and 1993, concrete blocks were dropped from helicopters to stop lava near Zafferana Etnea. The 2001 and 2002 lava flow destroyed visitor centres and the Etna Sud cable car post.

① Circumetnea Train
From Catania, this narrow-gauge private railway passes Adrano (site of a Saracen bridge), Bronte (with several pistachio farms), Randazzo (to see Lake Gurrida and lava flows) and Linguaglossa (site of an open-air mural museum).

② Hiking
Hikes on lower slopes and towards the crater are possible, safety permitting. Tourist offices provide maps as well as guides.

Mount Etna

⑩ ⑤ ⑥

Linguaglossa

Maletto

Bronte

⑨

Milo

Giarre

Zafferana Etn

③

Adrano

Nicolosi

Pozzillo

Acireale

Paternò

Aci Castel

Catania

⑦

①

NEED TO KNOW

MAP G3 ▪ www.
visitsicily.info/etna

Parco dell'Etna: 095
821111; www.parco
etna.ct.it

Circumetnea Train: 095
541111; www.circum
etnea.it

AST Bus: from Catania to
Rifugio Sapienza Etna Sud;
leaves Catania 8:15am daily,
leaves Rifugio Sapienza
Etna Sud 4:30pm daily;
www.aziendasiciliana
trasporti.it

Guides: north Etna
(Linguaglossa), www.
guidetnanord.com; south
Etna (Nicolosi), www.
etnaguide.eu

▪ Rifugio Sapienza Etna
Sud *(www.rifugiosapienza.
com)* is a hotel, restau-
rant and pizzeria.

▪ Bring warm clothing in
case of a drop in temp-
erature, sturdy shoes and
glasses to protect your
eyes. For novice hikers,
joining a guided tour is
recommended.

④ Vegetation

Etna is home to a
variety of trees, from oak
and chestnut in lower
areas to pine and birch
higher up. Wild flowers,
including violets **(above)**,
flourish in the soil.

⑤ Slopes to the East and North

These slopes are home
to the *Betula aetnensis*
birch, unique to Mount
Etna, and, in Sant'Alfio,
the *Castagno dei Cento
Cavalli* (Chestnut of 100
Horses), one of the old-
est and largest trees in
the world. Lava flows
have formed caves and
grottoes, used as shel-
ters and ice stores.

⑥ Valle del Bove

This crater was
created by a collapse
of the volcano wall. It
covers 7 km by 5 km
(4.5 miles by 3 miles)
and has walls more than
1,000 m (3,000 ft) high.
In 1991 a vent opened,
releasing lava into the
valley for two years.

⑦ Slopes to the West and South

Small volcanic cones and
cultivated crops, notably
pistachio, cover the wes-
tern slopes. Recent lava
flows can be seen on
the southern slopes.

⑨ Summit Craters

The summit height is
constantly in flux due
to the mounting volcanic
debris ejected during
explosions and the
frequent landslides.

⑧ Fauna

Weasels, wildcats,
foxes **(above)** and birds
such as the peregrine
falcon survive in wooded
areas. The only fauna at
the top are ladybirds.

⑩ Lava Flows

Molten lava is
more than 500° C
(930° F). In some places,
the constant flow, 2 m
(6.5 ft) underfoot, causes
the snow to melt.

Dramatic slopes of Mount Etna

🔟 ⭐ Syracuse

Founded in 733 BC by Corinthian settlers, Syracuse was one of the first Greek colonies on the island. It commissioned buildings and works of art, and founded sub-colonies, extending its territory through warfare to become the strongest city in the Mediterranean. The ancient city was several times the size of Syracuse today and was divided into five zones: Epipolae, Akradina, Neapolis, Tyche and the original settlement of Ortygia.

① Castello Maniace
Situated at the tip of Ortygia, Castello Maniace is a fortress (above) commissioned by Frederick II. Its 13th-century interiors are almost perfectly intact.

② Altar of Hieron II
Hieron II built this vast altar, the largest in Magna Graecia, around 225 BC and dedicated it to Zeus Eleutherios, the god of freedom.

③ Catacombs of San Giovanni
Throughout these vast limestone catacombs are burial chambers of various sizes to accommodate children, adults or families.

④ Latomia del Paradiso
Stone from this *latomia* (quarry) was used for the construction of Syracuse. Within the quarry is the *Orecchio di Dioniso* (the Ear of Dionysius) cavern (below), which was probably named because it has a large opening that resembles a human ear.

NEED TO KNOW

Altar of Hieron II, Latomia del Paradiso, Greek Theatre and Roman Amphitheatre: **MAP H5**; Via del Teatro Greco; 093 166206; summer: open 8:30am–6:30pm daily (ticket office: to 4:30pm during Greek theatre season); adm €10

Catacombs of San Giovanni: **MAP H5**; Largo San Marciano 3; 093 164694; open from 9:30am daily (closing hours vary, closed for lunch); adm €8

Museo Archeologico, Syracuse: **MAP H5**; Viale Teocrito 66;

093 1489511; open 9am–6pm Tue–Sat (to 1pm Sun & hols); adm €8

■ The Neapolis Archaeological Zone includes the Altar of Hieron II, Latomia del Paradiso, Greek and Roman Amphitheatres.

■ Combined tickets (€13.50) are available for the Museo Archeologico, Syracuse and the Neapolis Archaeological Zone.

■ When touring archaeological sites, leave artifacts untouched and intact for future generations to enjoy.

Syracuse

↑ ⑩ 8 km (5 miles)

1 km (0.6 miles)

2 km (1 mile)

3 km (2 miles)

VIALE RIZZO
VIALE TERACATI
VIA C. REIMANN
VIALE AUGUSTO
VIALE TEÓCRITO
TYCHE
NEAPOLIS
V. GIUSEPPE TESTAFERRATA
VIA L. LUIGI CADORNA
PIAZZA VITTORIA
CORSO GELONE
VIALE PAOLO ORSI
PIAZZA REPUBBLICA

ARCHIMEDES

The renowned inventor, mathematician and engineer Archimedes (287–212 BC) was born in Syracuse. Among his important discoveries is the Archimedes Principle, the study of an object's displacement of its own weight in water. He put his other inventions, such as catapults and pulleys, to use in war when he was military advisor to King Hieron II.

⑤ Greek Theatre

Begun in the 6th century BC, the Greek Theatre **(above)** became the largest in Sicily. Many of the tragedies written by Aeschylus were first staged here.

⑥ Roman Amphitheatre

This Roman arena was built during the 3rd century AD and is one of the largest of its kind, built by local stonemasons.

⑦ Museo Archeologico, Syracuse

Also known as Museo Archeologico Regionale Paolo Orsi after the archaeologist Paolo Orsi, this museum *(see pp26–7)* displays artifacts that he found in Syracuse.

⑧ Temple of Minerva

The city's 18th-century Baroque cathedral *(see p47)* incorporates an ancient temple of Minerva, which had been built over the site of a monument to Athena.

⑩ Castello Eurialo

The castle is the most important extant Greek military installation in Sicily. It was built by Dionysus the Younger in the 5th century BC, and improved by Hieron II.

⑨ Temple of Apollo

Dating back to the 6th century BC, this is the oldest Doric temple **(above)** still standing in western Europe. The base has an inscription to the god Apollo.

Museo Archeologico, Syracuse

Archaeological finds from the necropolis of Pantalica

1 Material from Pantalica

Pantalica, near Palazzolo Acreide, was inhabited by the pre-Greek Sicels, who produced elegant red-glazed pottery.

2 Bronze Age Material from Castelluccio

Materials from the Castelluccio site, between Noto and Palazzolo Acreide, such as bowls, cups and jugs, show trade links between early Sicilians and eastern Mediterranean cultures.

3 Mother Goddess

From the Temple of Megara Hyblaea, this object made of terra-cotta represents the mother goddess nursing twins. Known in Italian as Madre Dea, she is known for a remarkable sense of solidity blended with tenderness.

Museum Archeologico, Syracuse

[floorplan diagram with numbered markers 9, 7, 1, 2 on left; 5, 3, 10, 8, 6, 4 on right]

Key to floorplan
- Ground floor
- First floor

4 Villa Landolina Gardens

These gardens sit on a site that is rich in finds from locations including an ancient Greek necropolis, parts of Hellenistic streets and Christian catacombs.

5 Greek Kouros, Lentini

This 6th-century-BC *kouros* (statue of a muscular youth) is one of the best examples of ancient Greek sculpture.

6 Gela Vase Collection

A *lekythoi* (tall one-handed vase) painted with *Herakles and the Hydra* is the most impressive.

7 Venus Anadyomene

A Roman copy of a Greek 2nd-century-BC original. From her pose to the polish of the marble, she is the epitome of a mythical goddess.

8 Ephebus at Adrano

This small athletic bronze figure of an *ephebus* or adolescent was found near Adrano, and dates from around 460 BC.

Bronze statue of Ephebus

THE HISTORY OF ANCIENT SYRACUSE

Under the tyrant Gelon, Syracuse formed a mighty alliance with other Greeks at Akragas (Agrigento) and Gela to defeat the Carthaginians at Himera in 480 BC. Hieron I (478–466 BC) and Dionysius (405–367 BC) made Syracuse the most powerful city on the island and in the Mediterranean. In 413 BC Athens sent a fleet in the "Great Expedition" to put down the threat, and with help from Sparta, the Athenians were defeated. Despite their warlord image, Syracuse's rulers were patrons of the arts – Hieron II (265–215 BC) expanded the great theatre and Aeschylus, Pindar, Plutarch and Plato were present at court. After Hieron II's death, however, Syracuse sided not with Rome but with Carthage in the Second Punic War. After a siege lasting two years, Syracuse fell to Rome in 212 BC and began a slow decline.

5th-century bust of a woman made in colourful terracotta.

Museo Archeologico, Syracuse has many remnants of the mighty colony of Syracuse, including sculpture and everyday objects.

TOP 10
COLONIES OF ANCIENT SYRACUSE

1 Akrai (Palazzolo Acreide)

2 Kasmenai (Casmene)

3 Kamarina (Camarina)

4 Adronan (Adrano)

5 Thermae (Termini Imerese)

6 Cephaloedium (Cefalù)

7 Katane (Catania)

8 Tauromenium (Taormina)

9 Zancle (Messina)

10 Selinus (Selinunte)

⑨ Temples of Athena and Apollo

Fragments from two Doric temples on Ortygia are on show, such as polychrome parts of a Gorgon.

⑩ Wooden Statuettes of Demeter and Kore

These rare examples of wooden statuary were found at a sanctuary between Gela and Agrigento. They date from the late 7th century BC and survived because they were covered in the mineral-rich mud of a local spring.

Terracotta relief showing a Gorgon

TOP 10 ⭐ Noto

After the massive earthquake that destroyed almost all of eastern Sicily in 1693, major reconstruction resulted in cities and villages being designed in the Baroque style, then at the height of its popularity. Noto is one of the best examples of the form. Designed specifically to include vistas of the countryside, the urban plan was also sensitive to the needs of the citizens. The soft, locally quarried stone adapted well to the carved decorations, but, unfortunately, the elements have taken their toll on it and renovations have been necessary.

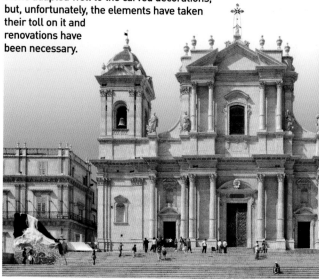

1 Cattedrale di San Nicolò

Noto's splendid Baroque cathedral **(above)** sits on top of Labisi's grand staircase. San Nicolò was built in stages throughout the 18th century, with input from architects Gagliardi and Sinatra.

2 Porta Reale

The Royal Gate **(left)** was erected in 1838 to greet King Ferdinand II. It offers a grand entrance to Noto's main street, Corso Vittorio Emanuele.

3 Chiesa di San Francesco

The 18th-century church of San Francesco has a Baroque portal, stucco interior and a wooden statue of the Virgin Mary.

4 Chiesa di Montevergini

An elegantly simple church, with a concave façade, marks the end of Via Nicolaci. Nearby is Palazzo Nicolaci, with its decorated balconies **(above)** supported by carved grotesques.

Chiesa di San Domenico

Gagliardi's masterpiece (1737) has an exuberant, convex façade, filled with niches and columns creating dramatic contrasts of light and shade.

San Carlo al Corso

Built in 1730, this church has various ceiling paintings **(left)** and a graceful concave façade. Wonderfully elegant columns on the façade progress from Doric to Ionic and finally Corinthian. A vertiginous climb to the top of the *campanile* (bell tower) provides beautiful views over the town.

NEED TO KNOW

MAP G5

Cattedrale di San Nicolò: open 9am–1pm & 3–8pm daily

San Carlo al Corso: Corso Vittorio Emanuele; open 10am–8pm daily (to 10pm Jul & Aug); adm (bell tower)

■ Sample Sicilian pastries and *gelati* at Caffè Sicilia *(see p80),* located on the Corso next to San Carlo.

Piazza Municipio, Palazzo Ducezio

The lovely town square is home to the Palazzo Ducezio **(above)**, now the town hall, designed by Sinatra in 1742. A loggia runs along the façade.

Palazzi, Via Cavour

Via Cavour is lined with *palazzi* of noble families. The Palazzo Trigona is a stately Baroque design of 1781 with characteristically curved balconies and a frescoed interior. On the corner to the left lies Palazzo Battaglia, which is a late Baroque work by Gagliardi.

Chiesa di Santa Chiara & Santissimo Salvatore

On opposite sides of the street are the convent of Santa Chiara and the monastery of Santissimo Salvatore. Santa Chiara's oval interior houses a 16th-century *Madonna and Child* sculpted by Sicilian Antonello Gagini.

Old Market, Via Rocco Pirri

Noto's lively market was at one time held in this courtyard, but butchers and bakers have now been replaced by boutiques. However, there is a market with fresh local produce in town every Monday across from the church of San Domenico.

BAROQUE ARCHITECTURE

The Baroque style grew out of the Renaissance, which used Classical forms and primary shapes to create balance and proportion. Baroque architects applied these forms to curved and ovoid shapes to achieve movement and drama. Typical features include an elliptical floorplan, a façade that projects outward or undulates, the use of light and shade, concave forms, as well as plenty of exuberant decoration.

🔟 ⭐ Villa Romana del Casale

As the hunting lodge of an important Roman official (perhaps Maximianus, Diocletian's co-emperor), the villa at Piazza Armerina was decorated with what is now the best preserved and most extensive set of Roman mosaics in the world. The lavish villa was constructed over a period of more than 50 years from the late 3rd century to the early 4th century AD, and its airy rooms, peristyles, thermal baths and gardens with pools and fountains were laid out on four natural terraces.

② Narthex of the Thermae

The long narthex in the thermae (gym) is decorated with a circus scene. Horse-drawn chariots careen around a track, in the centre of which is an image of the obelisk of Constantinus II.

Villa Romana del Casale

① Arion and Naiads

The floor of this living room, which had marble-faced walls, is decorated with a lively scene of the bejewelled Arion playing a lyre **(above)**. She is surrounded by naiads.

NEED TO KNOW

MAP F4 ▪ Contrada Casale, 6 km (3.5 miles) from Piazza Armerina ▪ 093 5680036 ▪ www.villaromanadelcasale.it

Open 9am–7pm & 8–10:30pm daily

Adm €10

▪ It gets hot inside the villa's wood and plexi-glass structure. Bring water to stay hydrated.

▪ In the summer, a courtesy minibus runs from Piazza Armerina.

③ Private Apartments

The floors of the family's private apartments **(above)** are decorated with the scenes of a children's hunt. Panels throughout depict foliage, flowers and baskets of fruit and vegetables.

④ Ten Girls in Bikinis

Perhaps the most famous mosaic in the villa is the bikini-clad athletes. They appear to have just finished a competition: the winner has been awarded a flower crown and a palm sceptre.

7 Great Hunting Scene

These mosaics show two countries (personified) surrounded by sea. The array of animals on land and in the sea includes lions, elephants, tigers and a leopard attacking a gazelle **(left)**.

10 Triclinium

The triclinium, used for banqueting, opens on one side onto a lovely garden surrounded by an elliptical portico. The mosaics are of a grand scale, in keeping with their subject, the Ten Labours of Hercules.

5 Xystus

On the northern side of the xystus, the elliptical garden off the triclinium, are three rooms decorated with scenes of the *vendemmia* (grape harvest).

6 Aqueduct

Near the entrance to the villa are remains of the aqueduct **(below)**, which provided water for the baths, fountains, gardens and household.

8 Public Room off the Peristyle

The reception room is decorated with a hunting scene **(above)** – one of the earliest mosaics in the villa. Hunters and dogs chase beasts, spear a wild boar and carry it away on their shoulders.

9 Changing Room for the Thermae

Here the emperor's family is shown: his mother, daughter and son, accompanied by enslaved persons carrying their equipment for the baths and gym.

MOSAICS

The stunning mosaic floors of Villa Romana are almost perfectly preserved as a result of the house being buried under a mudslide in the 12th century. The mosaic artist was highly skilled, forming large-scale images from millions of little polychrome tiles known as *tesserae* to cover 3,500 sq m (37,670 sq ft) of floor space.

🔟⭐ Agrigento and the Valle dei Templi

Aligned with Syracuse, Greek Akragas was one of the most important towns in Sicily during the Greek period. It constructed temples to its gods, and was known for breeding horses, with which it consistently won the Olympic Games. After being besieged by the Carthaginians in 406 BC, the town was taken by the Romans in 261 BC, renamed Agrigentum, and remained in Roman control until the fall of the Empire. The ruins of the ancient Greek city are now known as the *Valle dei Templi* (Valley of the Temples).

③ Centro Storico
Pass through the historic centre to get to the Duomo. The route takes visitors from Via Atenea via alleyways and passes artisans' workshops and locals pausing from their daily errands to chat.

① Temple of Herakles
Amid olive and almond trees lie the ruins of this hexastyle temple **(above)** dating from around 500 BC. Cross over the ancient street and walk over the stones to see the *cella* wall and Doric columns – beautiful at sunset.

④ San Nicola
The front of the church has an interesting 13th-century portal that reuses materials from a Roman ruin, and a nicely arched interior.

② Temple of Castor and Pollux
Considered a symbol of Sicily and also known as the Temple of the Dioscuri, this temple **(below)** features four lone columns and entablature that were put together from pieces of other temples in the 19th century.

5 Temple of Olympian Zeus

All that remains of this temple is a copy of one of its giant statues (above). The original is in the Archaeological Museum.

Agrigento and the Valle dei Templi

6 Temple of Hera

Patches of red at this temple to the queen of the gods (c 450 BC) are fire damage, perhaps from the Carthaginian siege of 406 BC.

7 Greek Roads, Gates and Walls

Walking from temple to temple through the valley, visitors can see what is left of the Greek city: rutted roads and walls bearing marks from later ages, when gaps were carved into them for new Byzantine tombs.

8 Abbazia di Santo Spirito

The resident Cistercian nuns at this 13th-century abbey still practise the old tradition of pastry-making, once the exclusive work of the convents.

9 Hellenistic/ Roman Quarter

Among knee-high ruins are door jambs in walls, basins, columns, mills, steps, remains of the drainage system and mosaic flooring.

VALLE DEI TEMPLI GUIDE

The site is divided into three sections, all near a central car park with ticket booth and tourist information office. The Temple of Olympian Zeus and the Sanctuary of the Chthonic Deities are in an area just to the west of the car park. The entrance to the temples along the Via Sacra (Hera, Herakles and Concordia) is across the street. Up the Via dei Templi you will find the Hellenistic/ Roman Quarter and the Museo Archeologico, Agrigento (see pp34–5).

10 Temple of Concordia

The hexastyle Temple of Concordia (below) has remained intact because it was converted for use as a church. It dates from 430 BC.

NEED TO KNOW
MAP D4

Valle dei Templi: 0922 1839996; open 8:30am–10pm daily (to 11pm in summer, Sun & hols); adm €12

Museo Archeologico, Agrigento: Contrada S Nicola 12; 092 2401565; open 8:30am–11pm Mon–Fri (to midnight Sat, Sun & hols); adm

combined ticket €17; www.parcovalledei templi.it

San Nicola: Via Passeggiata Archeologica, 20

▪ Avoid the crowded restaurants at the temple site and have a meal in town (see p123).

▪ The temples are spectacular at night, when the buildings are floodlit.

Museo Archeologico, Agrigento

Museo Archeologico, Agrigento

Key to floorplan
- Basement
- Ground floor

temples, just above the cornice, to funnel rainwater to the ground. Note that they were painted in bright colours, as were all of the elements of the temple above the level of the column capitals.

3 Model of the Temple of Olympian Zeus

This scale reconstruction of the Temple of Olympian Zeus (see p33), the largest known Doric temple in the world, allows visitors to appreciate the once enormous size of the building. Take note of the position of the 8-m- (26-ft-) tall *telamoni* (giant stone figures) in relation to the massive columns. More than twice as tallas these giant figures, the temple's imposing columns measured 16.5m (54 ft) in height and had a diameter of 4 m (13 ft) at their base.

1 Head of a Bull

Materials excavated from both Agrigento and Gela are found in the first two galleries. They include Bronze Age pots painted with red geometric designs, locally produced pottery, as well as Greek finds. One of the most interesting is the little head of a bull, hand-moulded in pinched terracotta.

2 Lion-Head Waterspouts

Recovered from various sites at Agrigento (including the temples of Herakles and Demeter), these spouts, shaped like lions' heads, were originally placed along the roof of

Marmorean sarcophagus

4 Sarcophagus of a Child

This sarcophagus, dating from the 2nd century BC, was only discovered in the 1970s. The panels, carved in high relief, vividly illustrate scenes from the child's life. There is a detailed scene of the sick room, showing the father pulling his beard in mourning.

5 Roman Quarter Mosaics

These particularly fine Roman mosaics from the 2nd century AD are made of tiny tesserae (tiles). They served as centrepieces to the decorative mosaic flooring of houses in the residential sector of the city.

Display of carved waterspouts

The collection of vases at the Museo Archeologico, Agrigento

6 Vase Collection

The vase collection includes outstanding examples of Attic black-figure and red-figure vases as well as Hellenistic vases. The *krater* (a tall vase with a sturdy base and two handles), with a rare white background, shows the figures of Perseus and Andromeda.

7 Ephebus of Agrigento

Described as an *ephebus* (a youth taking part in a religious rite), this beautifully carved marble figure illustrates the transition from the static archaic style to the severe style. Note the fine modelling of the boy's musculature and the movement of the figure, which dramatically contrasts to the almost Egyptian-like stilted and stiff figures of the former archaic style.

8 Greek and Roman Helmets

Discovered in Eraclea Minoa, the fascinating Greek battle helmets are designed with ear holes, while the Roman ones have a topknot and finely chased rims.

9 Red-figure Krater

The "Battle of the Amazons" (c 460 BC) design on this striking *krater* vase has been attributed to the Niobid painter. The artist skilfully created space on the curved surface by illustrating fallen bodies, bows and arrows, and other battlefield paraphernalia in rough perspective.

The main scene shows Achilles killing an Amazon queen (and falling in love with her as he does so).

10 Telamone and Telamone Heads

Thirty-eight *telamoni* once supported the entablature of the Temple of Olympian Zeus. A complete figure was reconstructed in the 1800s from various parts found on the site. Each of these figures was composed of numerous stones, covered with a smooth stucco overlay, and probably colour as well. Scholars still debate the exact form and position of the *telamoni*, but it may be that they stood with their feet splayed.

Giant telamone figure

TOP 10 ⭐ Selinunte

The ruins of ancient Selinunte *(Selinus)*, once a large settlement at the westernmost reaches of Magna Graecia, loom high on a promontory above the sparkling Mediterranean. Selinunte was founded around 608 BC and enjoyed centuries of prosperity before being reduced to rubble by the Carthaginians during the First Punic War. Now one of the most important archaeological sites in Europe, it is home to one of the largest Greek temples in the world.

1 East Group of Temples

Here lie the ruins of three temples **(above)** on which decorative fragments are identifiable. Temple E is an example of balanced Doric order.

2 Temple G

The only octastyle temple at Selinunte (all others are hexastyle), Temple G **(below)** is one of the four largest Greek temples in the world. Its columns are more than 16 m (52 ft) high. It was left unfinished in 480 BC.

3 Temples A and O

Temple A and Temple O, of which only the bases remain, are identical. They were built in Doric style around 480 BC, which makes them the most recent ruins on the Selinunte site.

4 Acropolis

The promontory was levelled by the first settlers, allowing them to build sacred buildings; commercial and residential structures followed.

5 Temple C

Built on a rise, this was the most important temple on the site. It was decorated with polychrome stone and terracotta elements.

6 Fortified Walls of the Acropolis

The original walls, built of large blocks of stone, were reinforced after the city was sacked by Carthage in 409 BC, and a second circle built around 305 BC.

8 Metopes

The metopes **(left)** at Selinunte, carved panels showing scenes from Greek mythology, are now in the Museo Archeologico Regionale Antonio Salinas *(see p92)*. The metopes from temples E and F are outstanding examples of Classical style.

THE ORIENTATION OF SELINUNTE

Selinunte was built on hilltops around the mouths of the Cotone and Selinon (now the Modione) rivers. From the main car park, along the ticket booth, a path leads to the East Group of Temples. The Acropolis is located across the valley (the location of the old harbour) and is accessible on foot or by car; the site's second car park is located at its base. The sanctuary of Malophorus, reached by walking west from the Acropolis, cannot be accessed by private cars.

9 North Gate

Of great importance for the defence of Selinunte, the 7-m- (23-ft-) high North Gate was protected by a sophisticated fortification of three bastions and a double line of walls. After sustaining damage in 409 BC, the earlier ring of walls was reinforced.

10 Sanctuary of Malophorus

This funerary sanctuary is dedicated to Malophorus, who was the pomegranate-bearing goddess. The elegant piece **(left)** was in use from the 7th to the 3rd centuries BC.

Selinunte

9
EAST GROUP 1 2
7
ACROPOLIS
P
i
P
10
MARINELLA
400 metres
(437 yards)
5 6 3 4

7 Commercial Area and Stoa

Behind Temple D you can see the remains of shops, each with two rooms, a courtyard and stairs that led to the shopkeepers' apartments on the upper floors.

NEED TO KNOW

MAP B4 ▪ Marinella di Selinunte, SS 115 south of Castelvetrano ▪ 092 446277 ▪ www. selinunte.gov.it

Open 9am–6pm

Adm €6 (free adm for EU citizens under 18)

▪ Marinella beach offers a stunning view of the ruins.

▪ The tourist office at Castelvetrano organizes site tours in golf carts.

▪ Have a picnic dinner amid the ruins while enjoying dance or music. Details are available at the ticket booth.

▪ Free entry for journalists and people working in the archaeological field.

Features of a Doric Temple

1 Proportion
Greek architecture followed rules of proportion to ensure the beauty and harmony of the finished structure. Doric temples were built with a length-to-width ratio of 3:1 or 2:1. Column height was related proportionally to base diameter, with columns gradually becoming more slender over the centuries.

2 Columns
Doric columns have a simple capital and a fluted shaft without a base. The shaft is larger in diameter at the bottom than at the top.

5th-century BC altar at Temple A

5 Altar
A carved block of stone used for animal sacrifices was placed outside temples at the eastern end.

6 Frieze
This is the decorative feature of the entablature. It is made up of alternating triglyphs – grooved blocks ending in *guttae* (little teeth) – which support the structure above and metopes (broad panels usually carved with figurative scenes).

Fluted Doric columns

3 Colonnade
When columns are arranged around the outer edge of a temple's *crepidoma* (base), they form a colonnade. "Peripteral" refers to a single colonnade and "dipteral" to a double colonnade.

4 Pediments
The triangular gables above the entablature on a temple's short sides are the pediments, usually decorated with figures or reliefs.

Entablature and column

7 Roof
Roofs were made of wooden beams and terracotta tiles. They often had polychrome decorations such as gargoyles cast into the shapes of animals' heads, which functioned as waterspouts.

8 Colour
The architectural elements and sculpted pieces, particularly the parts of the entablature and the pediment, were always painted in bright colours (polychrome) – most typically in red, blue, white or yellow.

9 Cella
Each temple housed a *cella* or a sanctuary, usually an enclosed room in the centre of the temple. Here the sacred image or statue of a god or goddess was kept.

10 Entablature
The entablature rests above the capitals and below the pediment.

THE RISE AND FALL OF SELINUS

Selinus, which was named after the abundant wild celery (selinon) that still grows in the area, enjoyed prosperity and power with a sprawling urban complex of 80,000 inhabitants, impressive temple compounds, their own mint and extensive agricultural holdings. Located on the edge of Greek territory, Selinus was forced to fight border wars with Segesta and was in constant danger from attack by their mighty Carthaginian allies. Although it gradually accepted some Carthaginian influence and even declared itself neutral in the Battle of Himera (480 BC) between the warring Carthaginians and Syracusan Greeks, it preferred to remain a Greek ally. Selinus lost that right in 409 BC, when Hannibal and his forces sacked the town, forcing all inhabitants to abandon the residential sector. From then until its demise, Selinus was restricted to the refortified Acropolis and remained under Punic control. Selinus was finally abandoned in 250 BC, when Carthage, fighting Rome during the First Punic War, moved all residents to its stronghold at Lilybaeum (modern-day Marsala). A small community was located at Selinus during the Christian era, but it too was eventually abandoned and all knowledge of the town, even its name, was lost until archaeologists uncovered it in the 19th century.

Gelon's triumphal entry into Syracuse
is shown in this painting by Giuseppe Carta (1853). Gelon, king of Syracuse, saw off the Carthaginians at the Battle of Himera (480 BC).

**TOP 10
FINDS FROM
SELINUNTE**

1 Punishment of Acteon (470 BC)

2 Efebo (bronze statue, 470 BC)

3 Zeus and Hera (470 BC)

4 Perseus and the Gorgon (c 560–550 BC)

5 Statue of a Kore (6th century BC)

6 Tumminìa Wheat

7 Europa and the Bull (6th century BC)

8 Corinthian Oinochoe (6th century BC)

9 Attic Lekane (6th century BC)

10 Bronze Zeus (6th century BC)

Metope depicting Perseus beheading Medusa

The Top 10 of Everything

**Christ Pantocrator,
Monreale Cathedral**

⁑⓾ Moments in History

1 Ducetius
Ducetius unified his people, the Sicels of eastern Sicily, against the Greeks in 452 BC. He succeeded in fortifying positions and redistributing land until suffering final defeat at the hands of Syracuse.

2 Supremacy of Syracuse
The Syracusan tyrants Hieron I, Gelon and Dionysus I assured the ascendancy of Greek Sicily, with Syracuse at the helm. The Greek colonies fought among themselves, but united when it was necessary, including to defeat the Carthaginians at Himera in 480 BC.

Silver coin depicting winged victory

3 Roman Rule
Rome's successful siege of Syracuse in 212 BC marked the end of Greek power on the island. After centuries of warfare, Roman rule brought peace. *Praetors* were sent to Sicily to govern, including Verres, later prosecuted by Cicero for his misdeeds. Verres was the first in a long line of foreign plunderers.

4 Arab Invasion
After Byzantine rule for three centuries, the North African Moors invaded in AD 827 at Mazara del Vallo. They captured Palermo, made it their capital and turned it into the cosmopolitan city it remains today. They improved rural infrastructure and irrigation, and introduced new methods of agriculture and fishing.

5 Count Roger
Norman crusader Roger de Hauteville (also known as Count Roger or Roger I) took Sicily between 1061 and 1091. He was the first of a century of Norman rulers *(see p13)* who marked a significant turning point in the island's complex multicultural history.

6 The Sicilian Vespers
After decades of rule by the French Angevins, in 1282 an uprising began in Palermo. Having successfully instigated revolt and done away with the unpopular foreign sovereign, Sicilians invited Peter of Aragón to become their king.

Norman fleet of Roger de Hauteville in the 11th century

7 Unification

Centuries of misrule, foreign domination and the feudal system meant wealth, power and land fell into the hands of the few. Popular revolts began in 1820, reached a head in 1848, and in May 1860 the Italian socialist Garibaldi, with the aid of Sicilian Redshirts, took the island and convinced the peasant class to vote for Italian Unification.

Garibaldi leads the expedition

8 Emigration

After Unification, Sicily found itself highly taxed and ignored as an outpost of a "foreign" government. Peasant farmers were unable to feed their families and there was no sign of improvement. Such poverty led to the mass emigration to the Americas in the late 1800s and early 1900s.

9 Earthquakes

In 1908 an earthquake killed over 70,000 people and levelled more than 90 per cent of Messina. Another damaging quake, in 1968, left scores of villages destroyed in the Belice valley. Thousands were housed in shelters for 15 years, waiting for the government to resolve the problem.

10 The Maxi Trial

The conviction of 350 *mafiosi* during the 1980s led to the murder of the judges Giovanni Falcone and Paolo Borsellino in 1992. Notorious boss Giovanni Brusca was released from prison in 2021, causing outrage throughout Italy.

TOP 10 MYTHOLOGICAL FIGURES

1 Aeneas
Aeneas fled Troy, found refuge on Sicily, and founded Erice and Segesta.

2 Demeter
Goddess of agriculture, the harvest and fertility. Her cult was based in Enna.

3 Persephone
Demeter's daughter was taken by Hades into the underworld at Lake Pergusa.

4 Hephaestus (Vulcan)
The god of fire lived on Mount Etna, forging his father Zeus's lightning bolts with the flames of the volcano.

5 Odysseus (Ulysses)
The Greek military leader wandered the Mediterranean for 10 years trying to get home. Many of his adventures took place in Sicily.

6 Polyphemus
The giant shepherd Cyclops held Odysseus hostage in his cave in Mount Etna.

7 Aeolios
The King of the Winds and master of navigation lived on the Aeolian Islands.

8 Arethusa
Chased by the river god Alpheus, Arethusa threw herself into the Ionian Sea and sprung up at Syracuse, transformed into a fountain.

9 Acis
Murdered by the jealous Polyphemus, Acis was reincarnated as a river and gave his name to nine towns on the Ionian coast.

10 Scylla and Charybdis
These hideous sea monsters dwelled on either side of the Straits of Messina, terrorizing passing sailors.

Relief of deities and their horses

🔟 Ancient Sites

1 Syracuse
The Greeks founded a colony here in 733 BC and began a project of development and expansion that led to Syracuse *(see pp24–7)* becoming the most powerful city in the Mediterranean. Remains of defensive structures and sacred, social and residential areas are visible today. A comprehensive archaeology museum helps to make sense of the varied ruins.

Remains of a Greek temple, Selinunte

2 Solunto
This small village *(see p102)* was under Carthaginian control, along with Motya and Palermo, until it was taken by the Romans around 250 BC. The urban grid pattern still remains and the paved streets are lined with residences and shops, some with traces of ancient wall decoration, mosaics, columns and cisterns. The latter were of supreme importance because Solunto's position on a promontory above the Tyrrhenian Sea did not offer any natural water sources.

3 Taormina
Situated on Monte Tauro, the 3rd-century BC Greek theatre at Taormina *(see pp18–19)* is the second largest in Sicily, but ranks first for the beauty of its backdrop. The view of Reggio di Calabria, the Ionian Sea and Mount Etna is broken only by the *scena* – marble-faced niches and columns added later by the Romans.

Greek theatre, Taormina

4 Selinunte
This archaeological park *(see pp36–9)* protects the ruins of eight massive temples, including one of the largest known temples of the ancient world, Temple C. There are also remains of Phoenician, Carthaginian, Greek and Byzantine settlements.

5 Morgantina
Morgantina was an important commercial centre along the trade route from the north coast of Sicily and the Aeolian Islands to the south. Deep in Sicani and Sicel territory, this city *(see p117)* flourished during the Hellenistic and Roman periods, and extensive ruins date from that time.

6 Segesta
This peaceful and beautiful site *(see p100)* comprises the ruins of one of the most important cities of the Elimi, the Hellenized Sicani peoples, and one of the most perfect Doric temples ever constructed. The temple's purpose is unknown, adding mystery to the already ethereal site.

7 Agrigento

In the grounds of the Valle dei Templi lie Greek temples, and a sanctuary to the goddesses Demeter and Persephone, the so-called Rock Sanctuary. The medieval centre of the town *(see pp32–5)* is almost buried by modern development, though fascinating pieces of Greek structures were incorporated into it.

8 Villa Romana del Casale

The remains of this luxury hunting villa *(see pp30–31)* for a Roman official hold the best extant Roman mosaic cycle in the world. The rich figurative and decorative designs adorn the floors of the villa.

Mosaic at the Villa Romana del Casale

9 Motya

The island city *(see p101)* in the lagoon between Marsala and Trapani was used from the 8th century BC by the Phoenicians to control shipping routes in the eastern Mediterranean. It became a Carthaginian stronghold until its destruction by Syracuse in 398 BC. Today, walls with fortified gates and towers surround the entire perimeter and there is a man-made harbour within the walls. Ancient paved roads, sacred and residential areas can also be seen.

10 Tindari

The ruins of ancient Tyndaris are remarkably well preserved. This town *(see p111)* was one of the last Greek colonies in Sicily, founded by the Syracusans in 396 BC. Features include the remains of a Roman villa and baths, and an amphitheatre.

TOP 10 ARCHITECTURAL STYLES

Palazzo dei Normanni, Palermo

1 Phoenician
The Phoenician rectangular block walls fortified the ancient cities of Erice and Motya and built the foundations of the Palazzo dei Normanni.

2 Greek
Doric temples and semicircular theatres are what remain from the years Sicily spent under Greek rule.

3 Roman
Aqueducts and lavish patrician homes embellished with mosaics are the most common examples of this style.

4 Arab Norman
The golden age of Sicily saw the blending of sharp northern arches and arabesque red-coloured domes.

5 Spanish Baroque
The arrival of the Jesuits brought intricate marble inlays *(intarsia)* adorning church walls and altars.

6 Late Sicilian Baroque
An innovation created after the 1693 earthquake, this style can be seen in sandstone *palazzi* with grand stairways and intricate embellishments.

7 Neo Classical
Greco-Roman revival style featuring frescoes with colours from Pompeii ruins.

8 Neo Gothic
The gilded façade of the Palazzo dei Normanni is a prime example of this 18th-century movement.

9 Art Nouveau
The ornate Villa Igea in Palermo was inspired by this exquisite floral arts movement.

10 Ventennio
Austere white buildings such as the central post office or the courthouse in Palermo remain from the Fascist era.

TOP 10 Places of Worship

Palermo's Byzantine masterpiece, La Martorana

1 La Martorana and San Cataldo, Palermo

These churches (see p91) are fine examples of Arab-Norman architecture. The former has the only known portrait of King Roger II. San Cataldo has its original exterior and interior.

2 San Domenico, Palermo

Sicily's most illustrious citizens are buried here (see p91), including physicist Stanislao Cannizzaro and painter Pietro Novelli.

San Domenico church, Palermo

3 Monreale

The monastery and cathedral of Santa Maria La Nova (see pp14–15) were founded by William II in 1174. His tomb, along with the tombs of his father, King William I, as well as mother, Queen Margaret, are in the south transept.

4 San Carlo al Corso, Noto

Dedicated to San Carlo Borromeo, this 18th-century church (see p29) is located on the Corso and forms part of Noto's dramatic Baroque skyline. Climb the tower, which houses three bells, for views of the town's historical centre.

5 Moschea di Tunisia a Palermo

MAP L4 ▪ Vicolo Gran Cancelliere 10 ▪ 091 321231 ▪ Opening hours vary

Given its long history of invasion (see pp52–3), Sicily has always been a cosmopolitan island, particularly in its capital. Palermo is home to places of worship for a number of faiths and includes a mosque – a reminder of its former Arab inhabitants. The mosque is housed within the former deconsecrated church of San Paolino dei Giardinieri – a location chosen for its unique orientation towards Mecca.

6 Cappella Palatina, Palermo

This masterpiece of Arab-Norman art celebrates both the Glory of God and Norman rule. Masses are said in the richly decorated chapel *(see p13).*

7 San Giorgio, Ragusa
MAP F5 ▪ Piazza Duomo ▪ Open 9:30am–12:30pm & 3:30–6pm daily

The cathedral of Ragusa Ibla is built on a rise in a wide tree-lined piazza in the old town. The undulating façade is typical of the architect Gagliardi, supporting a central tower, bulging columns and swirly volutes.

8 Cathedral, Syracuse
MAP H5 ▪ Piazza Duomo ▪ Open 9am–6:30pm daily (to 7pm Jul & Aug) ▪ Adm

This Catholic place of worship is set within a previous sacred site. Behind the Baroque façade, the structure of a Greek temple to Minerva has been adapted for use as a church.

9 San Nicola, Agrigento

This 13th-century church *(see p32)* is found within the Valle dei Templi. Taking on a majestic golden hue at sunset, its façade mixes Gothic motifs with ancient Roman columns. In a chapel on the right, there is a Roman sarcophagus.

Byzantine interior, Cefalù Cathedral

10 Cathedral, Cefalù
MAP E2 ▪ Piazza Duomo ▪ 092 1922021 ▪ Open 8am–6:45pm daily ▪ Adm (cloisters)

In 1131, after a stormy crossing, Norman King Roger II landed at Cefalù and, giving thanks to God, commissioned the cathedral now famous for its Byzantine mosaic decoration and its restored cloisters. The church *(see p110)* has two typically Norman square bell towers.

🔟 Castles

Impregnable walls of Castello Ursino

1 Castello Ursino, Catania
MAP G4 ■ Piazza Federico di Svevia ■ Open 9am–7pm daily (last entry 6pm) ■ Adm

Built around 1250, the once-moated castle has been used variously as a royal residence, the seat of parliament and a prison. It now houses the town's Museo Civico.

2 Castello di Lombardia, Enna
MAP E4 ■ Open 9am–8pm daily

One of the largest castles in Sicily was built by Frederick II in 1233 on this high point. Massive walls and six towers remain. The octagonal Torre di Federico II is the only fully original part standing.

3 Castello Ventimiglia, Castelbuono
MAP E3 ■ Open 9:30am–1pm & 3–6:30pm daily (to 8:30pm Jun–Aug) ■ Adm

In 1316 the Ventimiglia family built their fortified family seat atop an outcrop in the Madonie mountains. Within is the Chapel of Sant'Anna by Giacomo Serpotta (1652–1732).

4 Castello Normanno, Aci Castello
MAP G4 ■ Open 9am–1pm & 3–7pm daily (winter: to 5pm) ■ Adm

The castle is perched atop a black promontory, jutting out over the sea. Built by the Normans, it was covered by lava flows in 1169. It was rebuilt, then partially destroyed by Frederick II of Aragón in 1297. A stairway scales the side of the fortifications, giving access to the interior. The passages and chambers hold the archaeological collection of the Museo Civico.

5 Castello di Caccamo
MAP D3 ■ Open 9am–1pm & 3–7pm daily ■ Adm

This 12th-century Norman castle dominates the village and valley below. Pass through the mighty walls, walk among ramparts and visit the *Sala di Congiura* (Hall of the Conspiracy), where in 1160 barons plotted to overthrow King William I.

Caccamo castle and the village below

6 Castello Eurialo

The fortifications of this castle *(see p128)* date from 5th century BC. They protected the western access to Greek Syracuse. Archimedes added a drawbridge, trenches and catapults to protect the keep, entered through tunnels from the trench.

7 Castello di Lipari

MAP G1 ▪ Open 3–7pm Mon–Sat, 9am–1:30pm & 3–7pm Sun & hols ▪ Adm

Lipari's castle rock has been fortified for six millennia. The 12th-century Norman gate offers a passage through walls fortified by the Greeks in the 4th century BC and again by the Spanish in 1556.

8 Castello di Donnafugata

MAP F6 ▪ Open 9am–7pm Tue–Sat ▪ Adm

Donnafugata is a mix of architectural styles. The Arabs fortified the site around AD 1000; it then became a castle around 1300. In 1865 a Venetian Gothic loggia was added.

9 Castello di Venere, Erice

MAP B2 ▪ Via Conte Pepoli ▪ Open Apr, Jul, Sep & Oct: 10am–6pm daily; Aug: 10am–8pm daily ▪ Adm

This Norman castle is impressively sited on a sheer cliff face. Inside, the remains of Norman walls surround the ancient area sacred to Venus Erycina – stones from her temple were used to build the castle. There are also Phoenician and Roman ruins here.

Vertiginous site of Castello di Venere

10 Castello di Mussomeli

MAP E4 ▪ Caltanissetta, Messina ▪ Open 9:15am–12:45pm & 3:15–6:45pm Tue–Sat ▪ Adm

Built on an 80-m- (262-ft-) high limestone rock, this castle is a fine example of 14th-century Gothic architecture. It is considered to be nearly impenetrable due to the sheer drops and its thick crannied walls.

⭐10 Museums

Reliefs in the Museo Archeologico Regionale Antonio Salinas, Palermo

① Museo Archeologico Regionale Antonio Salinas, Palermo

Housed in a former palace, this museum *(see p92)* is dedicated to the famous archaeologist Antonio Salinas. The objects on display here were recovered from sites in western Sicily and show the development of art and culture from prehistoric eras to the Roman period.

② Galleria Regionale di Sicilia, Palazzo Abatellis, Palermo

The Catalan-Gothic palace *(see p91)*, built at the end of the 15th century, is now home to the collections of the former National Museum. Paintings and sculptures by Sicilian masters

The Triumph of Death, Palazzo Abatellis

span the 13th to 16th centuries, complemented by works by Italian and Flemish artists.

③ Museo Archeologico, Syracuse

An important museum of archaeology, the Museo Archeologico at Syracuse *(see pp26–7)* documents the ancient cultures and civilizations of both Syracuse and eastern Sicily.

④ Museo Mandralisca, Cefalù

MAP E2 ▪ Via Mandralisca 13 ▪ 092 1421547 ▪ Open 9am–12:30pm & 3:30–7pm daily (summer: to 11pm) ▪ Adm ▪ www.fondazione mandralisca.it

The archaeological finds exhibited here include ancient Greek and Arab vases. There is also an art gallery dedicated to Sicilian artists. Antonello da Messina's *Portrait of a Man* (1465) is among the artworks on display.

⑤ Museo Regionale di Messina

MAP H2 ▪ Viale della Libertà 465, Messina ▪ 090 361292 ▪ Open 9am–6:30pm Tue–Sat (to 1pm Sun & hols) ▪ Adm

This museum features architectural, sculptural and decorative fragments recovered from churches after the 1908 earthquake, as well as paintings and sculptures, including two artworks by Caravaggio.

6 Museo del Sale, Paceco

Housed in a restored windmill, exhibits here *(see p66)* trace each stage of traditional salt-making, from filling the saltpans with seawater, to evaporation, recovering, cleaning, storing and grinding the salt.

7 Museo Archeologico Regionale Eoliano, Lipari

Objects on display in this interesting museum *(see p17)* range from obsidian tools of the Neolithic period to items acquired through foreign trade, such as Etruscan red-glazed ceramics. There are also beautiful vases and masks from Greece that have survived from the days of Sicily's Greek occupation.

Traditional Sicilian puppets

9 Casa-Museo di Antonino Uccello, Palazzolo Acreide

The mission of Antonino Uccello was to preserve what he saw as the fast-disappearing culture of peasant farmers and the range of traditional handmade items they used. Exhibits here *(see p129)* include puppets, carts, the living quarters of a peasant home and tools, illustrating a unique aspect of Sicilian history.

8 Le Ciminiere, Catania

MAP G4 ▪ Viale Africa ▪ 095 4011929 ▪ Museo dello Sbarco: open 9am–5pm Tue–Sun ▪ Adm

Literally "the chimneys", this former sulphur works is now a lively cultural centre. Features include the Museo dello Sbarco, a moving reminder of the US and British landings in Sicily in 1943, a Museo del Cinema *(see p66)* and a traditional puppet theatre.

Stone head from Museo Archeologico, Agrigento

10 Museo Archeologico, Agrigento

Archaeological finds exhibited at this museum *(see pp34–5)* are from Agrigento and related cities. They reveal the Bronze Age, Hellenization and the Roman era.

🔟 Vestiges of Invading Powers

Aqueduct across the valley

1 Waterworks
The Greeks and Romans used aqueducts and water-powered mills, while the Arabs introduced land irrigation to the area.

2 Dialect
The 22 dialects around the island are a testament to the great overlapping of cultures over the centuries. Words still in use include *naca* (crib) from Greek, *giuggilena* (sesame) from Arabic and *travagliare* (to work) from French. In the town of Piana degli Albanesi, the locals speak Arbëresh, derived from 16th-century Albanian.

3 Place Names
Many place names are Italian versions of original Greek or Latin names. Erice was known as Monte San Giuliano until Mussolini went on a name-changing spree and adopted an Italian version of its original Greek name, Eryx. Arabic names remain in abundance – look for names with the prefixes "Calta", "Gibil" and "Sala".

4 Urban Plans
Modern towns often follow ancient street patterns. The area of narrow straight streets known as

la pettina (the comb) in Syracuse is left over from the Greeks. The tiny, winding streets of Palermo's old neighbourhoods such as La Kalsa, or the street plan of Castelvetrano, come from Arab settlements. Cefalù's system of parallel streets leading down to the sea is Norman.

5 Farming Techniques
The Arabs systematically farmed according to plant type, bringing about more flavourful and bountiful harvests – especially of olives, which yielded a better olive oil. Irrigated by the *gebbia*, a nearby water cistern, they also knew when to stop the water supply to citrus fruits to get a richer flavour.

Penne all'arrabbiata

6 Pasta
Fresh pasta, made of regular wheat flour, was produced in Italy as early as the Etruscan era. Dried pasta, which can be stored, was probably invented by the Arabs using Sicily's *semola*, a hard durum wheat flour.

7 Crops
The Spanish introduced tomatoes, potatoes, chocolate and the prickly pear cactus, or *fico d'India*; the Greeks brought olive trees and grapevines; the Arabs citrus fruits, sugar cane, date palms, pistachios, flax, cotton and mulberries.

8 Fishing Techniques

Sicily's age-old fishing techniques were adapted from Arabic methods. In the channel between Levanzo and Favignana, the fishermen still practise the *mattanza*, encouraging tuna through an increasingly narrow system of nets to the surface. Fishermen work together, chanting rhythmically to haul them aboard and to the shore. Near Messina, swordfish are spotted from a tall mast and after a struggle, the majestic fish are lifted into a boat called a *feluche*.

Erosion due to heavy rainfall

9 Erosion

The Romans began the deforestation of the island in order to export timber and make way for wheat plantations. Sicily now has few trees and the earth is washed away during heavy rains.

10 Fortified Towers

The Spanish protected Sicily's coastline by constructing more than 100 defensive towers. Messages were passed by fire signals.

Fortified towers along Scopello coast

TOP 10 INVADERS

Battle of Himera, Punic Wars

1 Greeks
The first Greek colony founded at Naxos in 734 BC displaced the inhabitants of Sicel.

2 Carthaginians
Carthage invaded repeatedly and many Punic War battles were fought over Sicily.

3 Romans
After years of warfare, Rome finally took Sicily following the fall of Syracuse back in 212 BC.

4 Byzantines
In AD 535 Sicily became part of Justinian's Eastern Roman Empire.

5 Arabs
The Arab conquest of the island began in AD 827 and was complete only in AD 902 with the fall of Taormina.

6 Normans
After 30 years of crusades, Count Roger de Hauteville (see p42) finally took Sicily in 1091.

7 Spaniards
Peter of Aragón was crowned King of Sicily in 1282, beginning nearly 440 years of Spanish domination.

8 Bourbons
Sicily was given to the House of Savoy in the 1713 Peace of Utrecht treaty, and swapped for Sardinia seven years later, thereby coming under Habsburg rule.

9 Italians
Garibaldi and his Redshirts invaded at Marsala in 1860, starting the campaign that ended with the Unification of Italy.

10 Allied Forces
On 10 July 1943, Allied Forces under generals Patton and Montgomery landed at Licata and Pachino, taking Sicily in 38 days.

🔟 Customs and Traditions

1 Hand Gestures

A Grand Tour author reported that Sicilians had been using hand gestures since the Greek invasion as a way of furthering resistance against foreign rule. Some of the common gestures you see mean: "She's pretty," "This tastes great," "Let's go," "I couldn't care less," "Do you want to stop for a coffee?", "Be careful," "That's not such a good idea," and even "His wife is cheating on him."

2 The Sicilian Cart

Once used for transport, these wooden carts are painted in bright colours and depict scenes from traditional Sicilian puppet shows. They often feature in local parades.

Decorated Sicilian cart

3 Festivals

Festivals for patron saints once offered the only chance for a holiday, and entertainment. Feasts (see pp86–7) were often in spring, giving farmers a chance to rest after the planting and to pray for a successful harvest. The *festa* was the one day everyone came in from the fields for religious processions, games, horse races, music and fireworks.

Sicilian *botte* full of bottles of wine

4 Wine

A glass of new wine is enjoyed with *i muffuletti* (round sandwich bread baked with fennel seeds and dressed with salt and oil) on St Martin's Day – usually strong, amber-coloured wine retrieved from the *botte* (barrel). Many families have at least enough grapevines for a yearly *botte* of wine, keeping it in the cellar, in the garage or any other cool spot they can find.

5 Proverbs

Sicilians always have a quip spoken in dialect. Examples include: *Cu' avi 'nna bona vigna, avi pani, vinu e ligna* (He who owns a good vineyard has bread, wine and wood); *Cu nun 'sapi l'arti, chiudi putia* (He who does not know his craft, closes his shop); *Soggira e nora calaru di n'celu sciarriannu*s (Mothers-in-law and daughters-in-law were sent from heaven and started fighting before they hit the ground); and *La soggira voli bene a la nora comu n'rizzu n'pettu* (Mothers-in-law love their daughters-in-law like a sea urchin in the bed).

6 Legends

King Roger's 12th-century French court poets told stories of Charlemagne and the paladins and the King Arthur cycle, which once included Sicily in its milieu. The paladins survive today as puppet theatre heroes (see pp68–9).

7 I Morti

All Souls Day on 2 November is a major celebration. Families visit the cemetery, where tombs have been rigorously tidied up and adorned with fresh flowers for the glory of the dead and for the approval of family members and anyone else passing. Relatives from the other world (or this world) leave children gifts, such as toys, *frutta martorana* (fake fruits crafted from almond paste) and *pupi di cera*, garishly coloured sugar dolls.

8 Olive Oil

On 11 November – St Martin's Day – families celebrate their new, thick, spicy, green olive oil by trying it on *i muffuletti*. If they don't have their own olive trees, families obtain a year's supply of olive oil from a relative or another trusted source, making sure to have a full *giara*, a waist-high terracotta storage jar.

9 La Befana

This craggy old woman who declined an invitation to join the Three Kings bringing gifts to Christ in the manger regretted her decision, set out on her own, and has been travelling the earth ever since with a large sackful of gifts. At Epiphany (6 January) she fills children's socks with presents if they've been good, or with coal (usually of the sweet, edible kind) if they've been bad.

10 Artisanal Fishing

Fishing is big business, but there are still artisanal fleets that use nets and homemade lobster pots to pay homage to the cultural heritage and fishing traditions of Sicily.

Repairing nets after a day's fishing

TOP 10 SUPERSTITIONS AND FOLKLORE

The picturesque Isola Bella

1 Creation of the Ionian Coast
Legend has it that Polyphemus *(see p43)* tossed hill peaks into the sea, forming the coastline between Mazzaro and Isola Bella.

2 Old wives' tale
Hanging paintings of birds in the house is considered bad luck as feathers are believed to cause illness.

3 Serving wine
In the Middle Ages, a flick of the wrist while pouring wine meant that the drink had been poisoned, so Sicilians avoid pouring wine backhanded.

4 Wedding traditions
Newlyweds are gifted with a broom to sweep away evil spirits and salt to be sprinkled in their new home to purify it.

5 Local healers
A *mago* or *maga* (witch doctor) casts spells, heals diseases and brews potions.

6 Food-related rituals
There are many food-related rituals in Sicily, for example, a loaf of bread must be placed right side up on the table.

7 Table manners
Sicilians avoid handing a knife or salt to another person directly. Instead, they place it on the table in front of them.

8 Leftovers
After supper, it is customary to leave some bread or wine on the table for spirits to enjoy.

9 Evil eye
Wearing a red or coral horn-shaped amulet is believed to ward off evil eye.

10 Springtime
It is believed that the return of Persephone *(see p120)* from the underworld each year marks the beginning of spring.

TOP 10 Artists, Writers and Composers

Late 19th-century illustration of the Greek tragedy _Prometheus Bound_

1 Aeschylus

The "father of Greek tragedy" (525–456 BC) was born near Athens but made extended visits to Sicily. Only seven of around 500 plays have survived, among them _Agamemnon_, _Oedipus_ and _Prometheus Bound_. Many of his plays were premiered in Syracuse's theatre _(see p25)_, where they are still performed.

2 Antonello da Messina

The Messina-born Antonello (c 1430–79) is one of the masters of Italian Renaissance art. He is known for detail, intriguing portraits and the luminous quality of his paintings achieved through his skilful use of oil paints, learned from the Flemish masters. Italian Renaissance artists adopted oils in his wake, making it the standard medium for the world's greatest masterpieces. Antonello works remain in museums in Cefalù, Palermo, Messina and Syracuse.

3 The Gagini Family

Domenico Gagini (d 1492) and his son Antonello (1478–1536) set the style for architecture and sculpture in Sicily during the 15th and 16th centuries. The Gagini combined Renaissance and Gothic forms to create uniquely Sicilian pieces.

4 Giacomo Serpotta

Born in Palermo, Serpotta (1656–1732) decorated Baroque interiors, creating an aesthetic transition between architecture and painting by covering the area with figures and scenes modelled in stucco.

Portrait of Vincenzo Bellini

5 Vincenzo Bellini

The composer (1801–35) was born in Catania, trained in Naples and is buried in Catania's cathedral. His successful early works led to commissions for La Scala in Milan. _The Sleepwalker_ and _Norma_ are among his most successful operas.

6 Luigi Pirandello

Born at Chaos near Agrigento, Pirandello (1867–1936) is known as the founder of 20th-century drama with plays such as *Six Characters in Search of an Author* (1921).

7 Giuseppe Tomasi di Lampedusa

Lampedusa (1896–1957) is the author of *Il Gattopardo (The Leopard)*, a portrait of Sicilian aristocracy pre- and post-Unification. It was based on the life of his great-grandfather and published posthumously.

8 Salvatore Quasimodo

Born in Modica, novelist and poet Quasimodo (1901–68) wrote anti-Fascist works in a political climate that made it necessary to disguise his message. He was awarded the Nobel Prize in 1959.

9 Renato Guttuso

Originally from Bagheria, Guttuso (1912–87) painted energetic Expressionistic canvases that illustrated Sicilian peasant life and spoke out against the Mafia and Fascism.

10 Leonardo Sciascia

Sciascia (1921–89) was a political essayist and novelist. Works such as *The Wine Dark Sea* give an insight into the complicated world of Sicilian thinking and Mafia culture.

Novelist Leonardo Sciascia

TOP 10 FILMS SET IN SICILY

Burt Lancaster in *Il Gattopardo*

1 Il Gattopardo
Luchino Visconti's 1963 film version of Lampedusa's novel stars Burt Lancaster.

2 Divorzio all'Italiana
Marcello Mastroianni is a Sicilian aristocrat seeking a divorce in Pietro Germi's 1961 comedy.

3 A Ciascuno il Suo
Adapted from a Sciascia novel, a look into the Mafia and life in 1960s Sicily, directed by Elio Petri in 1967.

4 La Terra Trema
Visconti's 1948 adaptation of Verga's *I Malavoglia*, the story of a fisherman's failed dream of independence.

5 The Godfather (Il Padrino)
Francis Ford Coppola's iconic Mafia saga was based on the book by Mario Puzo.

6 Cento Giorni a Palermo
Giuseppe Ferrara's 1983 film tells the story of policeman Carlo Alberto Dalla Chiesa, murdered by the Mafia after just 100 days on the job.

7 Kaos
A 1984 film adaptation of four Pirandello stories.

8 Cinema Paradiso
Giuseppe Tornatore's 1989 Academy Award-winning film takes a romantic look at growing up in a remote village.

9 Il Postino
Shot on Salina, this film is about a Sicilian postman whose life is turned around through his friendship with the Chilean poet Pablo Neruda (1994).

10 I Cento Passi
Marco Tullio Giordana recounts the life of anti-Mafia activist Peppino Impastato in this 2002 film.

TOP10 Villages

The picturesque Novara di Sicilia

1 Novara di Sicilia
MAP G2

This little mountain village is tucked between the Peloritani and Nebrodi mountain ranges. The medieval site has a crumbling Arab castle and the 16th-century Chiesa Madre with naive wood carvings on the altar.

2 Scopello di Sopra
MAP C2

This small village of fishermen was almost inaccessible until the road was built from Castellammare. Now the village is experiencing something of a tourist boom, but has retained the charm of a tiny fishing hamlet, and you will still see an old mariner with huge nets stretched the length of the piazza, repairing the gaps with an enormous needle.

3 Sambuca di Sicilia
MAP C3

Featuring lovely Baroque buildings, Arabesque alleyways and a valley of vineyards, Sambuca di Sicilia is easily one of the most picturesque towns in all of Sicily – and without many tourists. In particular, the ruins of Mazzalakar castle, set along Lake Arancia (Orange Lake) are worth a visit.

4 Palazzolo Acreide

Originally a Greek village called Akrai (a small Greek theatre remains), Palazzolo Acreide *(see p125)* is an enchanting village in the Hyblean mountains with an impressive range of historic sites to visit, considering its size. Most of what you see today is Baroque: the churches are spectacular, particularly the large Church of San Sebastiano and the tiny Church of the Annunciation with its ornate twisting columns.

5 Butera
MAP E5

High on a plateau overlooking fields out to the sea, Butera dates from the Bronze Age and has traces of Lombard in its dialect. Famous for its acres of vineyards, it supplies grapes to local and national winemakers.

6 Piana degli Albanesi
MAP C2

Nestled in the Sicanian hills, this town was founded in the 15th century by Greco-Albanian refugees and has retained its unique heritage. The locals speak in Albanian dialect and street signs are bilingual. Weddings here take place with traditional costumes and Byzantine Catholic rites.

7 Mezzojuso
MAP D3

The name of this village translates as "halfway down" – and it is halfway down the Madonie mountains. It has an Alpine rather than a Mediterranean feel. It was home to Greco-Albanian settlers, and the Basilian monastery was a hub of cultural activity; it now houses a library with antique books.

8 Petralia Soprana
MAP E3

The highest village in Madonie, at 1,147m (3,760 ft) above sea level, medieval Petralia Soprana feels untouched by the modern world, with vistas of the rolling mountains below.

Petralia Soprana atop the mountains

Winding stone streets of Erice

9 Erice

The charming town of Erice *(see p99)* has managed to keep much of its medieval charm intact. The buildings are all built of locally quarried white stone, adding to its lovely storybook appearance. The stones of the steep streets have characteristic patterns, worn over time.

10 Palazzo Adriano
MAP D3

In the heart of this fertile area, Palazzo Adriano is lofty and remote. In Piazza Umberto I are two churches, Catholic Santa Maria del Lume and the Greek Orthodox Santa Maria Assunta, built in the 1400s. The Italian film *Cinema Paradiso (see p57)* was set here.

Beaches

Isolated cove with rocky towers in the sea, near Scopello

1 Castellammare del Golfo
MAP C2

The beaches west of Castellammare are prettier and less populated than those to the east. There are beautiful coves with clear water – those with pebble beaches are spectacular in Lo Zingaro (see p100) and at Scopello Tonnara, with its rock towers and old boat ramp for sunbathing.

2 Mondello
MAP D2

This is Palermo's backyard. It is crowded with the seaside villas of Palermo's aristocracy and locals taking advantage of the beach, bars, *gelaterie*, restaurants and clubs. Mondello is not very popular

for swimming due to its shallow waters. However, it is ideal for other beach activities.

3 Eraclea Minoa
MAP C4

Below the ruins of this Greek city (see p118), a little seaside village comes to life in summer. The sandy beach is long, wide and open, and buffered by pine woods. At either end are two bars providing beach chairs and snacks.

4 Aci Castello
MAP G4

Here clear, blue water laps onto the black lava rocks just below the castle (see p48). Descend to the left, where a water polo court is set up in summer, or to the right to a wooden deck for sunbathing and diving.

5 Mazzarò & Giardini Naxos
MAP H3

The water at the two resorts below Taormina is a calm, brilliant blue. The cable car from Taormina descends to Mazzarò, a resort area with two pebble beaches lined with bathing spots and coves. The popular Isola Bella (see p18) lies nearby. Giardini Naxos (see p109) is a town with a port and long stretches of beach lined with hotels.

The lively Mondello beach

6 Lampedusa
MAP B6

The tiny islet Isola dei Conigli, off Lampedusa, and the bay in between have been set apart as a nature reserve for sea turtles who lay their eggs on the beach. The water is clean and shallow in the bay and the sands are white, but there are no facilities, so bring your own supplies.

7 Scoglitti & Donnalucata
MAP F5–F6

The sandy beaches along this southeast stretch of coast are long and wide and splashed with green-blue surf. There is very little tourist development, beyond small fishing villages including Scoglitti as well as Donnalucata, with their nice markets and good restaurants, and little seaside villages that come to life in summer, such as Marina di Ragusa.

8 Selinunte
MAP B4

A large sandy beach stretches to the east of the port and just below the temples *(see pp36–9)*. Bathing establishments offer beach chairs, watersports equipment, restaurants and bars. It tends to be crowded with students hanging out and sunbathing, but through the small pine wood to the west you'll find an open beach for families.

9 Pollara, Salina
MAP G1

This beach *(see p16)* has a crescent of large pebbles with a cliff backdrop. When the wind is high, Pollara disappears under the waves, even in summer. A *faraglione* (rock tower) pokes out of the sea. Bring food and drink or get supplies in the piazza.

Cliffs of Pollara Beach, Salina

10 Vendicari
MAP G6

A spectacular nature reserve with sandy beaches set around a 15th-century Aragonese tower. The pristine coast here offers a peaceful, natural experience. The park is covered with Mediterranean maquis, and its wetland habitat is a stop for birds migrating to and from Africa.

Following pages The rooftops in the Baroque town of Ragusa

Outdoor Activities

Hikers on an old lava flow

1 Hiking

There are great hikes all over the island, whether you're looking for a strenuous climb up a volcano, a long walk through the green hills of the interior or an exciting trek on trails clinging to the cliffs above the blue sea. Most nature reserves are *orientata* (orientated), meaning that they have marked trails that may be graded for difficulty. Lo Zingaro *(see p100)* has a good selection of trails, as do the parks of the Nebrodi and Madonie mountain ranges *(see p113)*. Hire a guide to explore Mount Etna, Stromboli or Vulcano.

Diving off the Egadi Islands

2 Golf

www.italygolfandmore.com
■ Il Picciolo Golf Club: www.ilpicciolo golf.com ■ I Monasteri Golf Resort: www.imonasterigolfresort.com ■ Verdura Golf & Spa Resort: www. verduraresort.com

There are several 18-hole courses in Sicily, often set in dramatic coastal locations. Some of the courses are part of a luxury hotel complex offering spas, culinary initiatives and cultural events.

3 Fishing, Favignana

You can't join in the traditional *mattanza* fishing ritual *(see p53)*, but you can watch it in progress if you happen to be there when the tuna are running. You can also hire a boat with a local captain for a day's fishing.

4 Swimming

The unspoiled, clear water off Sicily and the offshore islands is spectacular, and great for swimming. The shoreline has sandy or pebble beaches, private coves, grottoes and rock formations. Visitors should note that lifeguards are not always on duty.

5 Watersports

Diving and snorkelling are available with trained guides through diving centres in many places, such as Scopello and the Aeolian Islands, or snorkel on your own to enjoy the marine life along Sicily's shores. Beaches in touristy areas hire out pedal boats and windsurfing boards.

6 Horse Riding

Nature reserves such as Lo Zingaro, the Madonie and Nebrodi mountain ranges and Mount Etna are populated with small farms with horses for hire. Ask at the nearest hotel or check park leaflets for *ippoturismo* and *maneggio* (stables).

Cycling is a good way to explore

7 Cycling

Sicily has a steep terrain for cyclists, though it is a great way to sightsee in the quieter towns and many tourist offices offer free bike hire. Hiring a bicycle on the islands is a convenient way to get around.

8 Exploring Gorges

Natural gorges and canyons are great places for a hike and swim during the hot summer. Companies run tours to the gorges, often as part of a day-long hike. The gorges at Alcàntara, Cava Grande and Gole di Tiberio are especially good.

9 Boating

Sail your own, arriving at one of Sicily's many ports, or hire a boat and a captain for an insider's tour of hidden coves.

10 Skiing on Mount Etna

The depth of snow depends on underground lava flows, but there's enough of a base for winter skiing on the northern slopes of Mount Etna (see pp20–21). At Zafferana Etnea, Linguaglossa or Nicolosi ski hire, a ski school and lifts are available.

TOP 10 SICILIAN FLORA AND FAUNA

1 Sea Turtles
Rare sea turtles bury their eggs in the sands of the Pelagie Islands and the Belice Estuary.

2 Sanfratellano Horse
A species indigenous to the Nebrodi, descendant of ancient *Equus sicanus*.

3 Cirneco dell'Etna
The native dog of Mount Etna is a natural hunter who seeks small prey.

4 Cactus
The *fico d'India*, or prickly pear, thrives in Sicily's arid climate.

5 Dwarf Palm
This tiny palm flourishes in the northwest of Sicily; its fronds are preferred by craftsmen for weaving baskets and brooms.

6 Fennel
Bright yellow, fluffy green or tall and crispy brown, depending upon the season, it covers hillsides and springs up along the side of roads.

7 Agave
The low-growing aloe-like plant with curling spiky leaves puts out a central stalk that can reach up to 12 m (40 ft).

8 Thistle
The hearty, spiky plant pops up along roadsides and in fields with its bright purple flowers – not to be confused with cultivated artichokes.

9 Forests
The few remains of once-prevalent pine, oak, cork-oak and beech forests are now carefully protected.

10 Girgentana Goat
This breed from the Agrigento area has long, twisting horns and is bred specially for its milk.

Girgentana goats and kids

Children's Attractions

1 Puppet Theatres

Showing riotous re-enactments of crusader sword fights, puppet theatres *(see pp68–9)* encourage the audience to root for a favourite crusader. The puppets "speak" in Italian, or Sicilian dialect, but it's easy enough to follow the action.

Museo di Geologia "G G Gemmellaro"

2 Museo di Geologia "G G Gemmellaro", Palermo

MAP L6 ▪ Corso Tukori 131 ▪ 091 23864665 ▪ Open 9am–1pm & 3–5pm Sun–Fri (to1pm Sat) ▪ Closed 25, 26 Dec & 1, 2 Jan

Palermo's impressive geological museum fascinates children and adults alike with displays from its collection of over 600,000 artifacts and specimens. These include remains of the elephants that roamed Sicily in the Pleistocene era; a quartz crystal containing a drop of Mediterranean seawater over 5 million years old; the skeleton of a woman, known as Thea, dating from the late Stone Age.

3 Castles

Sicily's castles *(see pp48–9)* are rich in history and intrigue, with trapdoors, secret passageways, dungeons, spy windows and hidden places from which boiling oil was once poured onto the enemy.

4 Museo del Sale, Paceco

South of Trapani, the small salt museum is inside a windmill. Its fascinating exhibits show how the windmill transfers water from pool to pool and grinds the harvested salt. Work in the saltpans *(see p102)* is ongoing, and you can see each stage that turns sea water to table salt. There is a restaurant on site.

5 Museo del Cinema, Catania

MAP G4 ▪ Piazzale Rocco Chinnici, "Le Ciminiere" ▪ 095 4011928 ▪ Open 9am–5pm Tue–Sun; Jul & Aug: 10am–6pm Tue–Sun (last entry 5pm) ▪ Closed hols ▪ Adm

Catania's child- and adult-friendly museum celebrates the cinematic arts and its history. Educational and fun, exhibits retell the story of an enduring love affair between cinema and Sicily.

6 Etnaland, Belpasso

MAP G4 ▪ 095 7913334 ▪ Open late Apr–mid-Sep (hours vary, check website for details) ▪ Adm ▪ www.etnaland.eu

Sicily's top theme park has a full-size dinosaur park and plenty of water rides, including the Crocodile Rapids. There are rides for the youngest children, and others that will get the adrenaline flowing in even the most hardened theme park veteran.

Gentle rides for young children at Etnaland

⑦ Motya

The archaeological park on the island of Motya *(see p101)* requires a short boat ride across the lagoon (less than 10 minutes each way). The spacious park shows inquisitive kids how the Phoenicians and the Carthaginians lived.

⑧ Museo dell'Etna, Viagrande

MAP G3 ■ Via Dietro Serra 6 ■ 095 7890768 ■ Open 9am–12:30pm Mon–Fri by reservation

This interactive museum dedicated to Mount Etna *(see pp20–21)* uses 3D models and satellite images to explain volcanic phenomena in a fun and interesting way.

Studying volcanoes, Museo dell'Etna

⑨ Nature Reserves

Sicily's nature reserves are ideal to spot wildlife, picnic, swim or use the graded hiking trails. Mount Etna *(see pp20–21)* is always smoking, if not throwing red sparks into the air. Guides give an account of lava flow and the gift shops screen spectacular video footage.

⑩ Museo Leonardo da Vinci e Archimedes, Syracuse

MAP H5 ■ Via Vincenzo Mirabella 31, Ortygia ■ Open 10:30am–7pm daily ■ Adm

At this mueum, kids can learn about mechanics and kinetics through interactive scale models of machines that were invented by Da Vinci.

TOP 10 FAMILY-FRIENDLY ADVENTURE PARKS

Parco Avventura Etna

1 Parco Avventura Etna, Milo
Climb into treehouses and slide down chutes at this adventure park, or simply go for a walk, near Mount Etna.

2 Città del Mare, Terrasini
Home to the highest water slide in Europe, this park guarantees fun and relaxation for the whole family.

3 L'EcoCampus Casaboli
This adventure park near Palermo allows children to climb trees and rope ladders, and enjoy a picnic in the forest.

4 Parco Avventura Madonie, Petralia Sottana
This adventure park is the place to spend the day learning about nature while sharpening your acrobatic skills.

5 Agriturismo Bergi, Castelbuono
Spend the day enjoying a delicious meal at this farmhouse while kids learn about the day-to-day life on a farm.

6 Giardino Inglese, Palermo
In the heart of the city, this urban park features rides and a roller-skating rink.

7 Acquapark Sommatino
On long hot summer days, this waterpark is an ideal place to escape from the heat.

8 Bioparco di Sicilia, Carini
See dinosaur replicas, exotic animals and rare flora while learning about the dangers of extinction.

9 Nebrodi Adventure Park, Longi
Slide down ropes and learn about bird watching, then go for a walk in the fresh Nebrodi air.

10 Parcallario, Buccheri
Have an adventurous day in the Hyblean hills while learning about local flora and fauna.

🔟 Puppet Traditions

Puppet theatre in Monreale

1 Origins

There were puppeteers in ancient Syracuse, but the Opera dei Pupi, as we know it today, became popular in the 1800s. Puppet theatres provided entertainment for thousands of Sicilians – Palermo had more than 25 theatres where crowds watched stories of adventure and romance. Travelling puppet theatres drew huge crowds in villages.

2 UNESCO Intangible Cultural Heritage

To protect Sicily's unique folk art tradition, Opera dei Pupi was added to UNESCO's Intangible Cultural Heritage of Humanity list in 2008. Sicilian puppet theatres are often family-run affairs, crafting the *burattini* (puppets or marionettes) using methods passed down for generations.

3 Stories

Productions relate saints' lives, Shakespearean themes, stories of bandits and local farces. The most traditional subjects are derived from the epic poems of the Carolingian cycle, retold by Ludovico Ariosto in his 1516 *Orlando Furioso*. The Holy Roman Emperor Charlemagne and his paladins battle for Christianity against the Saracens and Turks.

4 Catanese School

Puppets of the Catania tradition are almost 1.5 m (5 ft) tall. Puppeteers manoeuvre the heavy puppets via a metal pole attached to the heads, moving their limbs with strings. The puppets' joints are fixed and the swords of the paladins are drawn. They inhabit a narrow stage with a long horizontal backdrop and are sometimes joined by live actors.

5 Palermitan School

Palermitan puppets are around 1 m (3 ft) tall. They are entirely handled by strings, have movable joints, can raise their face guards and draw their swords at will. They are easily manipulated and their sword fights are more lively. The stage of the Palermo-style theatre is a deeply recessed space with room for many characters and decorated scenery.

6 Festival di Morgana, Palermo

This international puppet festival, held in November, promotes traditional as well as contemporary puppetry, and brings together artists and theatre companies from around the globe.

Scene at the Festival di Morgana

7 "The Bad Guys"

Saracens and Turks wear baggy trousers and moustaches and bear shields with a crescent moon. Charlemagne's brother-in-law and arch-enemy Gano di Magonza tries to overthrow the crown. Sorcerer Malagigi plays both sides, helping and hurting the paladins' cause.

8 "The Good Guys"

The Holy Roman Emperor Charlemagne and his paladins wear armour and skirts. Orlando carries a shield with a cross. His cousin Rinaldo, a brave fighter, has a lion on his shield, as does his warrior sister Bradamante. Angelica, admired by both men, is usually at their side.

Puppets in their armour

9 Assedio a Parigi

In this very traditional story, Charlemagne, under siege by the Turks, sends Rinaldo to prepare the French army and another warrior to Rome to ask assistance from the Pope. Rinaldo defeats the Turkish leader. Malagigi prompts Orlando and Rinaldo to end their differences and face the Saracens in Paris. Orlando saves the day.

10 The Defeat of Roncisvalle and the Death of Orlando

In a famous tale, Charlemagne is tricked by his brother-in-law Gano and the paladins find themselves outnumbered. After putting up a noble fight, Orlando dies.

TOP 10 PUPPET PLACES AND PEOPLE

Handmade puppets

1 Museo Internazionale delle Marionette Antonio Pasqualino, Palermo
This museum (see p94) houses fine puppets, stages and sets.

2 Museo Civico dell'Opera dei Pupi, Sortino
The collection of the Puglisi family, *pupari* (puppeteers) for five generations.

3 Opera dei Pupi di Enzo Mancuso, Palermo
Opened in 1928 by Enzo Mancuso, this place (see p71) is now operated by his grandson.

4 Opera dei Pupi, Syracuse
The Vaccaro-Mauceri company has performed puppet shows here (see p71) for generations.

5 Teatro dell'Opera dei Pupi Mimmo Cuticchio, Palermo
Giacomo Cuticchio's legacy lives on through the work of Mimmo Cuticchio.

6 Marionettistica Fratelli Napoli, Catania
Gaetano Napoli founded the Catanese puppet theatre in 1921.

7 Mimmo Cuticchio and Virgilio Sieni
A performance uniting contemporary dance and puppetry.

8 Teatro dei Pupi Siciliani-Famiglia Argento, Palmero
The Argento family has been performing here since 1893.

9 Salamanca, Catania
Francesco Salamanca is a restorer and collector of Sicilian puppets.

10 Anna Cuticchio: First Female Puppeteer, Palermo
Mimmo Cuticchio's daughter, Anna, once owned a theatre and manipulated over 60 puppets.

🔟 Performing Arts Venues

① Teatro Antico di Taormina

Resting on the acropolis of ancient Taormenium and famed for its views, this Greco-Roman theatre (see p18) is a magnificent outdoor performance venue. Its programme begins with the Taormina Film Festival in early summer and the theatre also hosts concerts by international artists.

Ancient amphitheatre, Taormina

② Santa Maria dello Spasimo, Palermo

The open nave of Santa Maria dello Spasimo (see p96), also known as Lo Spasimo, is a venue for performances and film screenings. Music can be heard from the upper outdoor terrace as well, while artworks are on display in the covered exhibition space.

③ Archaeological Park, Selinunte

During August performances of Greek drama, classical and modern dance, and music are staged among the ruins in Selinunte's archaeological park (see pp36–7). Performances start at 9pm.

④ Teatro Massimo Bellini, Catania

MAP G4 ■ Via Perrotta 12

Catania's great opera house, named after local composer Vincenzo Bellini (see p56), opened its doors in 1890. The season of opera and concerts, including ballet performances and chamber music by the theatre ballet company, runs from October to June.

⑤ Teatro Massimo, Palermo

The Teatro Massimo (see p96) was built in the 1880s as a symbol of post-Unification Sicily by Neo-Classical architects Giovanni Battista Basile and his son Ernesto. Despite its grandeur and superb acoustics, the theatre fell into decline. After a massive renovation effort, the doors were reopened in 1997, and once again it is Palermo's premier venue for classical music, ballet and opera.

6 Opera dei Pupi, Syracuse

MAP H5 ▪ **Via della Giudecca 22**
▪ **www.teatrodeipupisiracusa.it**

Puppeteers Mauceri and Vaccaro direct traditional puppet shows in the Catania style *(see p68)*; as well as the lives of the saints, there are the Mauceri family's own productions. You can also watch puppets being made and restored in the family workshop.

7 Teatro Ditirammu, Palermo

MAP P4 ▪ **Via Torremuzza 6** ▪ **www. teatroditirammu.it**

This 52-seat theatre in Palermo's historic Kalsa district stages Sicilian folk music concerts. It also promotes shows of lively tarantella or heart-wrenching storytelling set to music throughout the city – outdoors in Piazza Kalsa, for example.

8 Opera dei Pupi di Enzo Mancuso, Palermo

MAP L1 ▪ **Via Collegio di Maria al Borgo Vecchio 17** ▪ **091 8146971**
▪ **www.mancusopupi.it**

The Mancuso family is known for working with Sicilian puppets since 1928, and young Enzo dedicates himself to breathing new life into the art. He makes puppets as needed, but his collection also includes vintage models that have been passed down.

Traditional puppet tale

Stage at the Greek Theatre, Syracuse

9 Greek Theatre, Syracuse

Classical works are staged in spring in Syracuse's ancient theatre *(see p25)*, including Aeschylus's tragedies, premiered here thousands of years ago. Daily performances take place from mid-May through to the end of June. The largest theatre of ancient Sicily is mostly intact and fits modern stage sets and seating.

10 Teatro Luigi Pirandello, Agrigento

MAP D4 ▪ **Piazza Luigi Pirandello 35**
▪ **www.fondazioneteatropirandello.it**

The ornate Agrigento civic theatre *(see p57)* was opened in 1880. The venue was dedicated to the playwright Luigi Pirandello on the 10th anniversary of his death in 1946. From November to May there are modern theatre performances and dance, as well as works by Pirandello.

🔟 Nights Out

Jazz club in Palermo

1 Clubs

Discoteche open up each summer, often under new names and management from previous years. Huge crowds of visitors mix with locals to fill up the open-air dance floors and bars. Look for posters for clubs, especially in towns and villages close to the sea.

2 The Piazza

In villages in summer when people stay inside during hot afternoons, families and friends sit in the piazza and eat *gelato* into the night. In touristy towns, the piazza has a pub atmosphere with live music and outdoor tables, such as the Caffè del Molo and Bar al Duomo at Cefalù.

3 The Passeggiata

The *passeggiata* (promenade) can be an afternoon or an evening activity. In summer, join the crowds on the promenades at Selinunte, San Vito lo Capo, Mondello, Marina di Ragusa, Palermo (Via Ruggero Settimo) and Catania (Via Etnea).

4 Associazione Culturale Palab, Palermo

This lively cultural centre *(see p96)* stages live music, comedy, theatre, dance, film and exhibitions of contemporary art and photography. There's a cocktail bar, pizzeria and restaurant.

5 Via Landolina, Catania
MAP G4

Via Landolina, near the Piazza Bellini, is lined with bars and clubs. La Chiave (Nos. 64–70) usually has a programme of live music and in summer organizes Landolina Live, a full slate of live rock, folk and jazz during June, July and August.

6 I Candelai, Palermo
MAP K4 ■ Via dei Candelai 65

This Palermo dive has been going strong since 1996. Popular as a venue for live acts, arts events and tango lessons, it's a favourite with students from the nearby university.

Pavement cafés near Piazza Olivella, Palermo

⑦ Agorà, Catania
MAP G4 ▪ Piazza Currò 1

This lively bar and restaurant owes its unique atmosphere to the cool stream of water flowing through its cave area. The site has been in use since ancient Roman times, and now it lies below Catania's youth hostel, in the centre of town, beside the fish market.

The lively Cantavespri restaurant

⑧ Cantavespri, Palermo
MAP M5 ▪ Vicolo Valguarnera 10 ▪ www.facebook.com/cantavespri

Set in a 16th-century patrician's palace, Cantavespri is a nightclub, restaurant and concept bar. It has a staff of mixologists, a rock 'n' roll vinyl collection and live music nearly every night.

⑨ Zo, Catania
MAP G4 ▪ Piazzale Rocco Chinnici 6 ▪ 095 8168912 ▪ www.zoculture.it

This arts and cultural centre is located in the same former sulphur works as Le Ciminiere (see p51). It hosts music, dance and theatre performances, and temporary exhibitions. There is a café and restaurant too.

⑩ Lapis
www.lapisnet.it

This free publication has complete listings of music, theatre as well as art events. Separate editions are printed in Palermo and Catania.

TOP 10 FEATURES OF THE PASSEGGIATA

1 The Walk
The key to the walk on the *passeggiata* is to do it very slowly.

2 See
Everybody checks out everybody else for everything from physical attributes to their fashion sense to how well behaved their children are.

3 Be Seen
Wear the latest fashions, whether Dolce & Gabbana catwalk originals or market-stall copies.

4 Spectator Sport
If you prefer, feel free to sit and watch the *passeggiata* go by. A table outside a café is the perfect spot.

5 Who
From babies in prams to teens to grandparents, to entire families, couples and groups of friends, this is an open event.

6 The Touch
Everyone holds hands or entwines arms with their walking partners.

7 Food
The only things the Italians consume while in motion are *gelato* or peanuts or similar small snacks.

8 Men with Earpieces
Mobile devices allow sports fans to stay abreast of the *partita* (football match) or Formula Uno motor racing.

9 By Car
Locals drive the *passeggiata* with the windows down so that they can chat.

10 When and Where
The prime time is Sunday afternoon or any day from dusk onwards. Walk around a piazza, down a *corso* or promenade, or anywhere people happen to gather.

Piazza IX Aprile in Taormina

🔟 Wines and Wine Producers

① Monreale
MAP C2

Monreale has produced fine wines for centuries from indigenous grapes, such as Perricone, Inzolia, and Catarratto, as well as Chardonnay. Try at the Calatrasi Principe di Camporeale or Sellier de la Tour.

Marsala wine in production

② Marsala

A fortified wine produced in Marsala *(see p101)* since the 18th century. A DOC *(Denominazione di Origine Controllata)* was awarded in 1986. Marsala is produced as Fine, Superiore (aged at least two years), Riserva (aged at least four years) or Vergine and Soleras (aged at least 10 years). From Inzolia, Catarratto and Grillo grapes, the wine is amber with a citrus flower and almond perfume.

③ Nero d'Avola

This is the classic Sicilian red, made from at least 80 per cent of grapes of the same name with added Perricone, and characterized by its intense ruby colour and flavour of aromatic herbs. It's produced over the entire eastern half of the island but the two largest producers are between Palermo and Cefalù: Regaleali and Duca di Salaparuta.

④ Artisan Producers

Many artisan producers are making great wines. Look out for COS, Fondo Antico, Occhipinti, Graci, Frank Cornelissen, Palari, Girolamo Russo, La Moresca and Terra delle Sirene.

⑤ Malvasia and Passito

Producers on Salina leave their Malvasia delle Lipari grapes to dry out on the vine or on mats to concentrate the flavours to make a dessert wine that is thick and sweet. Pantelleria's Zibibbo grapes are treated in a similar way, left on the vine until the flavours have condensed to make a dessert wine with intense tastes of dried fruits and vanilla.

⑥ Bianco d'Alcamo

Eighty per cent Catarratto with a dash of Damaschino, Grecanico and Trebbiano make up this dry and fruity white. Abundant production (more grapes are grown in Trapani than any other Sicilian province) made this the classic Sicilian white. The area from San Vito Lo Capo to Castellammare and inland to Alcamo and Calatafimi is under DOC protection.

Road through Alcamo vineyards

7 Regaleali
MAP E3

This estate has been in the Tasca d'Almerita family since 1830. Famous for traditional Sicilian wines, their reds, based on Nero d'Avola, include Regaleali Rosso and the Rosso del Conte; whites, mainly of Inzolia and their own Varietà Tasca, include Villa Tasca as well as Nozze d'Oro.

Regaleali's Nero d'Avola

8 Erice
This wine is from grapes in the Erice valley, and varieties run from white to red to sweet dessert (*passito*). One of the best is the Syrah from the Casa Vinicola Fazio winery.

Vineyards near the base of Etna

9 Etna Bianco and Etna Rosso
Sicily's first DOC was awarded in 1968 to the southern and eastern zone of Mount Etna, where the white grapes Cataratto and Carricante flourish. Reds, mostly the Nerello Mascalese, grow at the volcano's base.

10 Cerasuolo di Vittoria
The cherry-red, dry and fruity wine is made from an interesting blend of Frappato, Calabrese and Nerello grapes grown near Vittoria in Ragusa. Established producers are buying vineyards here to produce their own versions of Cerasuolo.

TOP 10 GRAPE VARIETIES

Bunch of Zibibbo grapes

1 Zibibbo
The grape of Pantelleria, used traditionally for the sweet *passito*, is now also popular for crisp white wines.

2 Nero d'Avola
This powerhouse Sicilian red grape is cultivated in the eastern half of the island.

3 Frappato
Cultivated in Ragusa province, the primary grape of Cerasuolo di Vittoria.

4 Grillo
A white grape indigenous to western Sicily and the basis of Marsala and other whites.

5 Inzolia
Also called Ansonica, a white grape found throughout western Sicily, used in Marsala and other wines.

6 Nerello Mascalese
Primary red grape grown on the slopes of Mount Etna, blended with Nerello Cappuccio to make the deep, spicy Etna Rosso.

7 Malvasia di Lipari
Responsible for the fragrant wines of Salina, rich in flavours of almond and candied fruits.

8 Catarratto
A white grape grown from Marsala to Alcamo, Salina and Etna. Its character changes depending on the microclimate.

9 Grecanico
White grape native to western Sicily and one of the primary components of Bianco d'Alcamo.

10 Pollico
The oldest variety known on the island, these white grapes are used to make Moscato wine.

🔟 Sicilian Dishes

Sardines stuffed with breadcrumbs and raisins

1 Fish and Seafood

There is always an excellent choice of fish and seafood in Sicily. Look out for *sogliola* (sole), *triglie* (red mullet), *pesce spada* (swordfish), *tonno* (tuna), *mazzancolla* (large sweet prawns), *aragosta* (spiny lobster), *sarde* (sardines), *polpo* (octopus), *calamaro* (squid) and *gambero rosso* (red prawns).

2 Caponata

Originally a fish dish, *caponata* was adapted by the *cucina povera* (kitchen of the poor) as a slow-cooked mix of aubergine (eggplant), tomato, celery, capers, olives, raisins and pine nuts, flavoured with vinegar and sugar, and topped with toasted almonds.

Lemon ice cream

3 Pasta

The amazing variety of pasta dishes available makes use of all the bounty that Sicily has to offer. A typical Palermitan dish is *pasta con le sarde* (with sardines, fennel, pine nuts, raisins and anchovies). The pasta itself, made with local durum wheat, is firm and full of flavour.

4 Spleen Sandwiches

It takes a lot of curiosity to choose to sink your teeth into this classic street food staple. The sandwich can be either plain (*schettu*, single) or topped with grated cheese (*maritatu*, married). More daring versions come with crunchy trachea bits.

5 Gelato

The reason Sicilian ice cream (*gelato*) is so special (see p110) is its base: a *crema* developed from Arab and Spanish culinary influences that is made with milk, or almond milk, as well as starch. It produces a rich, smooth and light dessert.

6 Cassata and Cannoli

These classic Sicilian desserts are made with lightly sweetened ricotta. In *cassata*, ricotta and sponge cake are covered with marzipan and decorated with candied fruits. *Cannoli* are fried pastry shells filled with ricotta, candied fruit and chocolate chips.

7 Meat

Excellent lamb and pork are produced in Sicily. Sausages are always spiced and made with *semi di finocchio* (fennel seeds), stuffed in narrow casings and formed into continuous coils.

Traditional Sicilian *caponata*

8 Panelle

Another snack food available from street vendors are these small squares of fried batter made from chickpea flour and a sprinkling of parsley, then topped with salt and lemon juice. They are often served in a sandwich.

9 Arancini

A Sicilian fast-food treat that is available in bars and from street vendors. Balls of rice are stuffed with a meaty tomato or vegetable *ragù* or with ham and cheese, rolled in breadcrumbs, and fried.

Tasty, round, golden *arancini*

10 Bread

Bread in Sicily is made from *grano duro* (semolina flour), and once baked it is dense and golden. The shapes are particular too, including braided loaves. Bread is used in main dishes – *mollica* are spiced and toasted breadcrumbs, used instead of cheese on top of pasta. Look for *sfincione*, similar to a thick-crust pizza eaten as a snack, and *focacce*, thin baked layers of dough filled with greens, sausage, ricotta or tomato.

Bread in an array of shapes

TOP 10 LOCAL PRODUCE

Sicilian blood oranges

1 Citrus Fruits
Excellent lemons (there is a small, sweet variety) and oranges (with numerous blood-red varieties) abound.

2 Cheese
Sicilian cheese comes from cow's or sheep's milk. Look for *primo sale* or aged *pecorino*, *tuma*, *caciocavallo* and *Ragusano*.

3 Ricotta
A cheese by-product used for sweet and savoury dishes. Available fresh, baked, or salted and aged (called *ricotta salata*).

4 Capers
From tiny buds to the huge *cucunci*, the best come from Salina and Pantelleria.

5 Vegetables
Amazing bounty awaits at market-places and restaurants. Don't miss the long skinny *cucuzza* (squash) and spicy red garlic.

6 Salt
Richly flavoured salt has been harvested from the sea near Trapani since Phoenician times.

7 Durum Wheat
The secret behind Sicily's flavourful bread and pasta. The countryside is covered with wheat fields.

8 Almonds and Pistachios
Eastern Sicily is known for its production of these high-quality and richly flavoured nuts.

9 Tuna
You'll find this fish preserved in oil and fresh in a variety of cuts.

10 Olives and Olive Oil
Millions of olive trees produce excellent-quality table olives and thick, green aromatic olive oil.

🔟 Restaurants

1 Majore, Chiaramonte Gulfi

It's worth the trek to Majore, perched on a hilltop with fine views over the Ragusa plains. This simple restaurant (see p131), in the back of a butcher's shop, has been serving the finest pork dishes since 1896, including a range of salami antipasti.

The simple interiors of Majore

2 Pocho, San Vito lo Capo

The terrace at Pocho (see p105) offers pretty views of Monte Cofano and the bay. The restaurant's owner, Marilú Terrasi, is well-known for her couscous, and the extensive wine list is made up of selected Sicilian labels.

3 Piccolo Napoli, Palermo

Arguably the best fish restaurant in town, Piccolo Napoli (see p97) serves up only the freshest catches of the day and pairs them with locally sourced ingredients. Start with a hearty portion of *linguine alle vongole*, followed by a main of *sarde a beccafico*, all washed down with a local white wine.

4 Ristorante Fidone Maria, Frigintini

Maria Fidone and her family can be found in the kitchen at their homely *trattoria* (see p131), preparing hearty Ragusan meals for dinner. Everything is made in-house, including the pasta, bread, olive oil and liqueurs. For a first course, choose the thick broad-bean soup (*lolli*) or homemade pasta. For a second course, try stuffed chicken accompanied by stuffed aubergines (eggplants).

5 La Cialoma, Marzamemi

In the great atmosphere of the piazza of Marzamemi, La Cialoma (see p131) occupies the ancient tuna fishery of Prince Villadorata's family. The name is a Sicilian term for the work songs sung by tuna fishermen of old. La Cialoma has a small menu and a big wine list. The food is fresh, simple and nicely prepared. Try the excellent marinated sardines or, in season, the simple and delectable tuna braised with laurel.

The piazza at La Cialoma

The minimalistic decor of Accursio

Lamb dish, Ristorante Duomo

⑥ Osteria Nero d'Avola, Taormina

Creative yet unimposing dishes of local fish come from the open kitchen. The chef, Turi, is a hunter, so look for game in season. He offers seasonal and local ingredients prepared well and without too many flourishes. This restaurant *(see p115)* also stands out for its reasonable prices, which is rare in Taormina.

⑦ Cantina Siciliana, Trapani

Chef Pino Maggiore serves Trapani's classic *kus kus al pesce* (fish couscous) at this contemporary restaurant *(see p105)* in the old Jewish quarter. He also offers pasta dishes, including the sublime *pesto alla Trapanese*, with tomatoes, garlic, almonds and basil, as well as mains and desserts. Try ricotta-filled *cassateddi* and the best Sicilian wines.

⑧ La Madia, Licata

The seven-course tasting menu at La Madia *(see p123)* is a culinary experience that merits the two Michelin stars. The inventive cuttlefish "egg", served with squid ink couscous, is a must-try.

⑨ Accursio, Modica

This Michelin-starred restaurant *(see p131)* is set within an old *palazzo* in the heart of Modica. The head chef uses the best of Sicily's land-based and seafood produce, then puts a modern twist on the classics. The *arancino*, for example, is stuffed with ricotta and prawns and served on a plate.

⑩ Ristorante Duomo, Ragusa Ibla

Chef Ciccio Sultano carefully selects ingredients for his traditional Ragusan dishes, but adds his own twist. In three small, bright dining rooms, every course is excellent. The two different tasting menus at this restaurant *(see p131)* let you try a bit of everything.

Pasticcerie and Gelaterie

① Verona & Bonvegna, Catania

MAP G4 ■ Via Asiago 60

Undoubtedly the best *pasticceria* and *gelateria* in Catania, and one of the very best in Sicily. You can watch the skilled pastry chefs at work, creating mouthwatering masterpieces such as little filled ricotta doughnuts and their famed *cannoli*. Takeaway only, and there may well be a queue.

② Cistercian Monastery, Agrigento

The nuns at the monastery of the Santo Spirito *(see p33)* still offer pastries from behind the grate. They may look like something you've seen at other shops, but take a bite and taste how special they are. Order ahead for the speciality, sweet couscous.

③ Pasticceria Russo, Santa Venerina, near Catania

MAP G4 ■ Via Vittorio Emanuele 105

Since 1880 the Russo family has been making Catanese pastries with fine local ingredients, such as honey, pistachios, almonds and oranges.

Elegant interior of Pasticceria Russo

Fruit pastries at Pasticceria Cappello

④ Pasticceria Cappello, Palermo

MAP J6; Via Colonna Rotta 68 ■ MAP J2; Via Nicolo Garzilli 19

The two branches of this patisserie sell among the best pastries in Palermo. The *setteveli* cake, featuring seven different-flavoured chocolate layers, is said to be an unmissable experience.

⑤ Pasticceria Artigianale Grammatico Maria, Erice

Maria Grammatico spent many years in the orphanage inside Erice's cloistered San Carlo monastery, learning the nuns' centuries-old recipes for their *dolci*, the sale of which provided their keep *(see p104)*. The sweets are the opposite of monastic life: colourful and luxurious. Try *sospiri* (sighs), *cuori* (hearts) and *cuscinetti* (little pillows).

⑥ Caffè Sicilia, Noto

MAP G5 ■ Corso Vittorio Emanuele 125

For more than a century, the Assenza family has been at work in the maze-like laboratory of the Caffè Sicilia. They hunt down the highest-quality ingredients in the region, working to preserve the Sicilian pastry-making tradition. They create pastries from the recipes of Noto's ex-monastery of Santa Chiara as well as from their own recipes, such as chocolates with carob, chestnut or sweet basil filling, *giuggolena* (sesame seed, honey and orange zest bar) and herb-infused honey.

⑦ Gelateria Stancampiano, Palermo

MAP D2 ■ Via Giovanni Campolo 94

It's worth the walk to get to this unassuming family-owned shop with the creamiest *gelato* in Sicily. The staff proudly offer rows and rows of traditional and seasonal flavours served in cones, cups and brioches.

⑧ Antica Dolceria Bonajuto, Modica

MAP G6 ■ Corso Umberto I 159

Fig-filled *nucatoli* and citrus and honey *torrone* are displayed in this small, elegant shop. Their chocolate is still made using the ancient Aztec method of working the cocoa with sugar and spices.

Treats at Antica Dolceria Bonajuto

⑨ Dolceria Donna Elvira, Modica

MAP G6 ■ Via Risorgimento 32

Elvira Roccasalva reproduces by hand the sweets formerly made by Modica's cloistered nuns. She also uses the best-quality ingredients from the region to create her own recipes: try the *carato*, made with carob flour, raisins and almonds.

⑩ Pasticceria Arturo, Randazzo

MAP G3 ■ Via Umberto 73

This pastry shop specializes in sweets made with local pistachios, Sicilian almonds and hazelnuts. Try the spicy pistachio pastries and excellent granita while sitting in the marble interior or outside, enjoying the view.

TOP 10 SICILIAN DESSERTS

Cassata with spring flowers

1 Cassata
Layers of sponge cake and ricotta cream covered with colourful marzipan and candied fruits (see p76).

2 Gelato
Try soft and creamy *gelato*, *zabaglione*, *semifreddo* or the solid *pezzo duro*.

3 Gelo di Melone
The delectable watermelon jelly is infused with jasmine essence and topped with chocolate chips.

4 Cannoli
Ricotta cream of different flavours in fried pastry tubes (see p76).

5 Frutta di Martorana
Marzipan sculpted and painted to look like real fruit or other edibles.

6 Biscotti della Regina
Hard biscuits rolled in sesame seeds.

7 Cassateddi
Fried pastry pockets filled with ricotta flavoured with chocolate, lemon or cinnamon, eaten at breakfast time.

8 Coseduce or Cuccidati
Traditional fig-filled biscuits that exist under various names in every part of the island. Elaborate versions are made for St Joseph's Day (see p86) and called *squartucciati*.

9 'Mpanatigghi
These Modican *empanadas,* imported by the Spanish Counts, are a pastry crust filled with chocolate, spices and ground beef.

10 Granita
Ice is added to flavourings such as jasmine, orange, wild strawberry or almond.

Orange granita

▣10 Specialist Shops and Areas

Catania's premier shopping area around Via Etnea

1 Palermo and Catania

On and around Palermo's Via della Libertà *(see p95)* and Catania's Via Etnea *(see p114)* you can shop in Italy's fashionable, classic stores for household linens, clothing, shoes and handbags. Both boulevards offer a mix of stores, boutiques and chic cafés.

2 Le Colonne, Taormina

Situated on Taormina's Corso, Le Colonne *(see p114)* sells elegant jewellery. The proprietor makes each piece crafted to her own design, inspired by antique and historical motifs. Chunky necklaces of heavy gold with precious gems and rings set with antique incised stones are all unique items.

3 Ceramiche d'Arte F.lli Soldano, Sciacca

MAP C4 ■ Piazza Saverio Friscia 15

Alongside shops selling Sciacca's traditional green, yellow and blue ceramic dishes, the Soldano family produces traditional ceramics and modern designs on tableware and tiles.

4 Ceramiche De Simone, Palermo

This shop *(see p95)* sells brightly coloured ceramics with designs of jolly peasant farmers and fishermen going about their daily tasks.

5 Silva Ceramica, Caltagirone

MAP F4 ■ Piazza Umberto I, 19

In a courtyard off the piazza, Silva Ceramica produces imitations of antique designs, including tiles.

6 Altieri 1882, Erice

Altieri *(see p104)* produces ceramics in traditional styles as well as with their own innovative designs. There are also pieces in gold, silver and coral made in the decorative arts tradition of the Trapani region.

Unique jewellery from Le Colonne

7 Farruggio Design, Catania

MAP G4 ■ Via Ughetti 3

The craft of jewellery making has been handed down from father to son at Farruggio. They are considered one of the finest goldsmiths in all of Italy.

8 Siculamente, Ragusa
MAP F5 ≡ Piazza Duomo 11

Run by three young Sicilian entrepreneurs, here you can buy "T-scierts", caps, buttons and such with intriguing designs full of anti-Mafia symbolism and sayings in Sicilian dialect. These include the fatalistic *Futtatinni* (Don't worry about it) or this romantic description of Sicily: *Unni l'aceddi ci vannu a cantari e li sireni ci fannu l'amuri* (Where the birds go to sing and the mermaids go to make love).

9 Enoteca Picone, Palermo

To call Enoteca Picone *(see p95)* a "wine bar" would hardly do it justice. Founded in the 1940s, it started life as a hole-in-the-wall that sold wine directly from the cask to the consumer, but now it is the place to go for its range of over 500 Sicilian, Italian and international wines. It's popular for pre-dinner drinks, where you can sample your choice of wine accompanied by a platter of local meats and cheeses.

"Non-Mafia" goods at Punto Pizzo Free

10 Punto Pizzo Free, L'Emporio, Palermo

This emporium is set in the heart of the city *(see p95)*. It sells traditional products, books and crafts gathered from shops around Palermo whose owners have banded together refusing to pay the *pizzo* (the infamous Mafia protection money). There's safety in numbers, but these people are still on the front line, and their courage cannot be overstated. Buy a T-shirt, support the cause.

TOP 10 LOCAL MARKETS

Produce at La Vucciria market

1 La Vucciria, Palermo
MAP M4
One of Palermo's oldest markets, where vendors really put on a show.

2 Trapani
MAP B2
Each morning fishermen arrange their catch along the wharf, pitching them to passersby.

3 Selinunte
MAP B4
A lively 7am fish auction.

4 Ballarò, Palermo
MAP L6
Palermo's most interesting market sells fish, produce and household goods.

5 Del Capo, Palermo
MAP J4
Step back into 19th-century Palermo in the Mandamento del Capo streets, crowded with farmers, housewives, butchers and every sort of meat.

6 Syracuse, Ortygia
MAP H5
Rows of mussels, cherries, almonds, lemons – or whatever is in season.

7 Sciacca
MAP C4
Monday to Friday, in the afternoon, fishermen sell their catch on the wharf.

8 Donnalucata
MAP F6
Each morning, under awnings along the wharf, fishermen sell their catch.

9 Catania
MAP G4
Catania's market is famous for the variety of fish and the rowdy vendors.

10 Impromptu Markets
All over Sicily, farmers sell their own produce, such as artichokes, lemons or cheese from the side of the road.

🔟 Sicily for Free

1 Roman Ruins, Palermo
MAP K6 ■ Within Villa Bonanno, Piazza della Vittoria

Not as extensive and lavish as the villa at Piazza Armerina *(see p30)*, this site nonetheless offers a glimpse into Roman daily life in the late 2nd century AD – with vivid mosaic floors, statues, spas and outdoor latrines.

2 Byzantine church in a Roman bathhouse, Catania
MAP G4 ■ Piazza Mecca ■ 095 7150 508 ■ Open 9am–1pm Wed & Sun; call to book on other days

A monumental complex dating back to the Romans encloses the remains of a lavish bathhouse, which a few centuries later became a Byzantine church. Try fresco spotting here.

3 Roman Odeon, Taormina
MAP H3 ■ Opposite Palazzo Corvaja

Not as famous as the Teatro Antico, the Roman Odeon is still a great spot to visit. Discovered by chance in 1893, it dates back to the Octavian era and was built on the remains of a temple.

4 The White Cliffs of Sicily
On the southern coast between Realmonte and Porto Empedocle, the limestone cliffs have been shaped into steps by the elements. Known as La Scala dei Turchi, they are a popular seaside destination.

The stately Villino Florio

5 Villino Florio, Palermo
MAP J3 ■ Viale Regina Margherita ■ 091 7025471 ■ Open 9am–1pm Tue–Sat & first Sun of each month

The Belle Epoque-era Villino Florio was destroyed by a fire. It has now been restored to its original splendour.

6 Caravaggio in Syracuse
MAP H5 ■ Santa Lucia alla Badia (Piazza Duomo) ■ Open 11am–4pm Tue–Sun

This Baroque church holds one of Caravaggio's greatest and largest works, *The Burial of St Lucy* (1608).

White cliffs of La Scala dei Turchi

7 Museo della Manna, Pollina

MAP E2 ▪ Piazza Duomo ▪ Open 10am–1pm daily & 4–7:30pm Thu–Sun

This museum is in the heart of the Madonie Mountains, where *manna* (a natural sweetener) is harvested from ash trees. It pays tribute to this centuries-old tradition and offers an insight into local farming and agricultural traditions.

 8 Regional Sights and Museums

First Sun of each month

The Greek Theatre at Syracuse, the Valle dei Templi in Agrigento and Palazzo Abatellis in Palermo are some of the sights that are free on the first Sunday of each month. Many municipal and local museums are free every day to under 18s and over 65s; always ask before entering.

Valley of the Temples, Agrigento

 9 Museo Archeologico Regionale, Licata

MAP E5 ▪ Via Dante 12 ▪ 092 2772 602 ▪ Open 9am–1pm Tue–Sat, 4–6pm Tue & Thu ▪ Closed hols

This small yet impressive museum houses artifacts dating back to prehistoric times, as well as a rich collection of local Greek and Roman finds. Keep an eye out for the Greek-era steel-and-gold jewellery.

 10 Sagre (food festivals)

Most towns hold an annual *sagra* – a celebration of speciality food, which is an opportunity to mix with the locals. The festivals in Bronte and Palermo (see p87) are great.

TOP 10 BUDGET TIPS

Ferry from Panarea Island

1 Take ferries instead of hydrofoils
Ferries are cheaper than the faster hydrofoils, and you can sit outside to take in the spectacular views.

2 Buy a day pass for the bus
A *giornaliero* (day pass) ticket allows travel on buses until midnight, including the 389 to Monreale.

3 Half-price admission tickets
A full-price admission ticket can often allow half-price entry to other places. Always ask if a site belongs to an association of museums.

4 Aperitivo rinforzato
These nightly happy hours offer buffet food with your drink. Plates of seafood, pasta and cured meats can substitute for dinner – at a fraction of the price.

5 Hire a bicycle in Palermo
The city's bike-sharing programme allows visitors to get around town and travel in areas closed to traffic. Drop-off points in 50 places (www.amat-pa.it).

6 Hop-on, hop-off buses
A hop-on, hop-off bus tour offers a cost-effective way to see as many sites as possible.

7 Buy produce at outdoor markets
Avoid supermarkets, where possible, and shop at the markets as the locals do.

8 Drink house wine
Ask for a carafe of *vino della casa* (house wine) instead of a whole bottle.

9 Street food
Staples such as *panelle* (chickpea fritters) and *arancini* (rice balls) are fast food in Sicily, with generous portions that end up being an entire meal.

10 Return long-distance bus tickets
Buy a return ticket for long-distance buses, as these are often discounted.

Feasts and Processions

Crowds at the festival of Sant'Agata, Catania

1 Sant'Agata, Catania
Early Feb

One of the earliest saints, Agata was martyred in Catania's Piazza Stesicoro. The bejewelled reliquary bust of the saint is paraded around town followed by a procession of ten men carrying large, golden candlesticks on their backs. Balconies are draped in fabrics, flags fly, candles burn and fireworks blast at dawn. A smaller festival takes place in mid-August.

2 Carnevale, Sciacca, Termini Imerese, Acireale
Feb or Mar

The narrow streets of these towns are packed with revellers for parades, parties and competitions. Papier-mâché floats satirize current events or figures of popular culture.

3 San Giuseppe, Belice Valley
18–19 Mar

St Joseph's Day is celebrated fervently in the west, especially in villages of Salemi and Poggioreale. Altars are constructed in homes, schools and public spaces, piled with ornate breads and traditional foods – but no meat, out of respect for St Joseph's poverty.

4 Good Friday, Noto
Mar or Apr

The Holy Thorn is taken through the streets with the black-veiled Grieving Madonna, whilst a drum keeps a somber tempo and a trumpet lets out a mournful blast.

5 Good Friday, Trapani
Mar or Apr

A solemn procession depicting the Passion of Christ. Tableaus are decorated with flowers and bands play funeral dirges in the streets.

Good Friday procession, Trapani

6 Easter Sunday, Castelvetrano
Mar or Apr

On Easter Sunday in Castelvetrano a celebration of Christ's Resurrection takes place in Piazza Carlo d'Aragona. The Festa dell'Aurora (Feast of Dawn) draws crowds to watch the statue of Mary, dressed in a black cape of grief, enter the square from one side, while Christ, wearing white, enters from the other. To a dramatic drumbeat, the two come together. Mary's black cape falls away to reveal a bright dress, music plays and everyone cheers.

7 San Sebastiano and San Paolo, Palazzolo Acreide

San Paolo: 29 Jun; San Sebastiano: early Aug

The landowners and farmers loyal to San Paolo and the merchants and artisans loyal to San Sebastiano try to out-celebrate each other with huge statues of the saints. Worshippers process barefoot well into the night.

Celebrations in Palazzolo Acreide

8 Santa Rosalia, Palermo

Mid-Jul

For six days the relics of Rosalia, which are said to have saved Palermo from the plague in 1624, are paraded around the streets on top of an ornate *vera* (float).

9 Festival of the Assumption, Randazzo

15 Aug

One of the most spectacular floats of all is paraded from Piazza di Santa Maria through the narrow streets to Piazza Loreto. The tall float carries young local boys dressed as angels, saints, Jesus and the Madonna.

10 Santa Lucia, Syracuse

Mid-Dec

A silver statue of Syracuse's patron saint travels from the Duomo to the Chiesa di Santa Lucia, while the faithful attach votive eyes to her image.

TOP 10 FOOD FESTIVALS ACROSS SICILY

1 Festival di Cannolo, Palermo
Early Apr
The art and tradition of the *cannolo* is celebrated at San Lorenzo market.

2 Sagra del Carciofo, Cerda
25 Apr
Artichoke festival; music in the piazza.

3 Mostra dei Formaggi della Valle del Belice e Sagra della Ricotta, Poggioreale
Late May or early Jun
Watch ricotta made in traditional and modern methods.

4 Festa della Ciliegia, Chiusa Sclafani
Early or mid-Jun
Cherry festival; traditional folk music.

5 Sagra della Cipolla, Giarratana
Mid-Aug
Savour dishes made with local flat, sweet onions.

6 Sagra delle Sarde, Selinunte
Late Aug or early Sep
A procession of the Madonna of the Fishermen and a sardine feast.

7 Couscous Fest, San Vito lo Capo
Last week in Sep
Chefs compete in an international couscous contest, with tastings.

8 Sagra del Pistacchio, Bronte
Late Sep–early Oct
A lively week-long festival dedicated to the tasty local nut.

9 Ottobrata Zafferanese
Every Sun in Oct
All over Zafferana Etnea, a fair of local wine, chestnuts, cheese and honey.

10 Sagra della Cassatella, Agri
Mid-Nov
A festival celebrating the sweet Sicilian delicacy *cassatella*.

Couscous festival

Sicily
Area by Area

Picturesque resort of Cefalù

🔟 Palermo

Settled by the Phoenicians in the 8th century BC, Palermo fell first to the Romans, then to the Arab invaders, who chose Palermo for their capital, making the city one of the most magnificent and powerful in the world. This splendour was compounded during the Norman reign, which brought a western influence to the island. Today the remains of earlier ages coexist with each other and with modern life: laundry billows off balconies of 15th-century palaces; buses rumble past even older buildings displaying a mix of east and west. Buildings destroyed in World War II have been left open to the sky, but Sicilians are ever resourceful: restaurants seat diners in crumbling, yet romantic courtyards, while a once-dilapidated church has a new role as an atmospheric arts venue.

Ancient Greek terracotta vessel

PALERMO

Central Palermo

1 Palazzo Abatellis
MAP P4 ■ Via Alloro 4
■ Open 9am–6:30pm Tue–
Fri (to 1pm Sat, Sun & hols)
■ Adm

Sicily's regional fine arts
museum *(see p50)* is housed
in a 15th-century palace.
Highlights include a fresco
of the *Triumph of Death*.

2 San Domenico Church, Oratorio del Rosario and the Vucciria

MAP M3 ■ Church of San Domenico:
Piazza S Domenico; open 8am–5pm
Tue–Fri (to 7pm Sat), 9am–1pm &
5–7pm Sun; adm ■ Oratorio del
Rosario: Via dei Bambinai 2; open
9am–6pm Mon–Sat

Bordering the Vucciria market *(see
p83)* to the north is the Church of

Church and piazza of San Domenico

San Domenico *(see p46)*, burial
place of notable Sicilians. Rebuilt
in the Baroque style in 1640, the
façade is 18th century. Behind the
church is the chapel, the Oratorio
del Rosario, with an altarpiece by
Anthony Van Dyck.

3 La Martorana and San Cataldo

MAP L5 ■ Piazza Bellini 3 ■ La
Martorana: open 8:30am–1pm
& 3:30–5:30pm Mon–Sat, 9–10:30am
Sun & hols; adm ■ San Cataldo: open
9:30am–12:30pm & 3–6pm daily

In Piazza Bellini there are two
splendid churches *(see p46)*.
The little mid-12th-century San
Cataldo has three Arab-style,
bulbous red domes in a row,
latticed windows and an elegant,
bare interior. La Martorana has
a Norman bell tower (c 1140),
a 16th-century Baroque façade
and original mosaic decoration.

Ceiling of La Martorana

Greater Palermo

0 km   2
0 miles   2

VIA DELLO OLIMPO
LUNGOMARE CRISTOFORO COLOMBO
VIALE DIANA
VIALE STRASBURGO
VIALE DE FANTE
E90
VIALE MICHELANGELO
VIALE LEONARDO DA VINCI
VIALE GIUSEPPE PITRE
CORSO CALATAFIMI
VIALE ERNESTO BASILE
V. MESSINA MARINE
SS624
VIA VILLAGRAZIA
SS186

See map left

4 The New City
MAP J1

The wide, tree-lined boulevard Via della Libertà travels west from the Teatro Politeama, where the modern city begins, full of shops and cafés. It passes the Giardino Inglese, laid out with palms, to Piazza Vittorio Veneto and Royal Park (La Favorita), once a royal hunting ground.

5 Albergheria
MAP K6 & L6

Bordered by Via Vittorio Emanuele and Via Maqueda, this rather run-down residential area is a maze of streets strung with billowing laundry. The heart of the neighbourhood is Ballarò Market (see p83). Don't miss the 17th-century Chiesa del Carmine on Via Giovanni Grasso, with its stuccoed interior and frilly, polychrome cupola.

6 Museo Archeologico Regionale Antonio Salinas
MAP L3 ■ **Piazza Olivella 24** ■ **Open 9am–6pm Tue–Sat (to 1:30pm Sun & hols)** ■ **Adm**

The museum displays finds from western Sicily, from the Neolithic age to the Roman period. Among Punic and Egyptian objects is the Palermo Stone (c 2700 BC), with a hieroglyphic inscription. There are also Greek vases, Roman sculpture, and Archaic and Classical metopes recovered from Selinunte (see pp36–7).

7 Quattro Canti
MAP L5

The heart of town is the intersection of Via Maqueda and Via Vittorio Emanuele. Called the Quattro Canti (the four corners that divide Palermo into quadrants), each is swathed in sculptural decoration. The town hall is in the Piazza Pretoria, although the square is more commonly known as the Piazza della Vergogna (Square of Shame), after the nude statues perched around the edge of the elaborate fountain, originally intended for a Florentine garden.

Boats moored at La Cala harbour

8 La Cala and Piazza Marina
MAP N3

Yachts in the port of La Cala can be seen from the 15th-century church of Santa Maria della Catena, while palaces line the Piazza Marina. In the centre of the gardens is a statue of Garibaldi (see p43). The 1582 Porta Felice leads out to the Foro Italico and the seafront, for waterside walks.

Façade of Palermo Cathedral

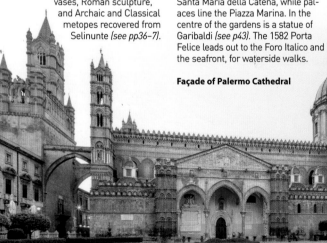

THE MAFIA

During centuries of absentee sovereign power, Sicilians distrusted government, built a loyalty to their own *(la cosa nostra)* and relied on justice given out by local bosses. After Unification (1860) landowners used thugs for protection and the underworld system thrived. Using crime to create fear and form alliances, the Mafia infiltrated society. Today, a grassroots network in Palermo, Addio Pizzo, pushes back against businesses paying bribes for protection.

⑨ La Kalsa
MAP N5 ▪ Bordered by Foro Italico, Via Lincoln, Garibaldi & Alloro

La Kalsa is the northeast quadrant of old Palermo, where the Arab population established their government offices. It was heavily bombed during World War II, but the once-derelict area has been gentrified in recent years. There are jewels to be discovered on nearly every corner: look out for the decadent Rococco-style Oratorio di San Lorenzo and the awe-inspiring and imposing Norman church La Magione.

⑩ Norman Palermo

The splendid Norman kingdom in Sicily was marked by a mix of cultures which is manifested in the buildings dating from the era *(see pp12–13)*. Palermo became a fine example of the best Norman architecture and decoration.Seek out the Palazzo dei Normanni and the Cathedral, which combine western and Arabic styles.

A MORNING IN LA KALSA AND ALBERGHERIA

▶ From Via Maqueda take the Piazza Santi Quaranta Martiri up to the **Chiesa del Gesù** *(Piazza Casa Professa 21)* for a look at the Baroque decoration of the interior. Beyond the church, enter the streets taken over by **Ballarò Market** *(see p83)* and spend some time making your way through the stalls. For a late breakfast, stop at one of the stalls serving *panelle (see p77)* or fried aubergine (eggplant) sandwiches.

From Piazza Ballarò, pass through the old neighbourhood and by the Chiesa del Carmine, with its colourful dome, and take the Via Case Nuove to Via Maqueda. Head into La Kalsa on Via Gorizia to Via Garibaldi, where you can still see parts of the magnificent original structure of the Palazzo Ajutamicristo. Continue down to **Santa Maria dello Spasimo** *(see p96)*, where there may be contemporary art on view. Take the residential Via della Vetreria to Via Alloro and the regional fine arts museum in **Palazzo Abatellis** *(see p91)* designed by Matteo Carnalivari.

Go south on Via Alloro until the Piazza d'Aragona and take a right turn into Via A Paternostro to the Piazza San Francesco. Have lunch at the **Antica Focacceria** *(see p97)*, sitting in the piazza under the Gothic façade of San Francesco, or in the marble and wrought-iron interior, where you can watch the chefs serving up Sicilian specialities such as *caponata (see p76)*. For dessert, there's always good *gelato* to be found at one of the *gelaterie* in the piazza.

See map on pp90–91 ←

The Best of the Rest

1 Porta Nuova
MAP J6

This imposing gateway to the city was erected in 1569 as a triumphal arch to commemorate Charles V's victory in Tunis.

Façade of the Porta Nuova

2 Castello della Zisa
MAP N2 ■ Piazza Zisa 1 ■ Open 9am–6:30pm Mon–Sun ■ Adm

The palace has stalactite-style ceilings, fountains, mosaic decoration and a collection of Arab art.

3 Palazzo Mirto
MAP N4 ■ Via Merlo 2 ■ Open 9am–6pm Tue–Sat (to 1pm Sun & hols) ■ Adm

One of the few surviving aristocratic *palazzi* in Palermo. The lavish interior has 18th- and 19th-century furnishings and allegorical frescoes.

4 Oratorio di Santa Cita
MAP M3 ■ Via Valverde 3 ■ 091 8431605 ■ Open Sep–Jul: 9am–1pm Mon–Sat ■ Adm

The interior of this chapel is covered with stucco decoration and Giacomo Serpotta's masterpiece (c 1600).

Boats docked on Mondello's port

5 Palazzo Belmonte Riso
MAP L5 ■ Via Vittorio Emanuele 365 ■ Open 10am–7:30pm Tue, Wed & Sun (to11:30pm Thu–Sat) ■ Adm

The Museum of Modern Art exhibits international and Sicilian artists here.

6 Galleria d'Arte Moderna
MAP M5 ■ Via Sant'Anna 21 ■ Open 9:30am–6:30pm Tue–Sun

Contemporary international art in a splendid convent.

7 Museo Internazionale delle Marionette Antonio Pasqualino
MAP N4 ■ Piazzatta A Pasqualino 5 ■ Open 10am–2pm Mon & Sun (to 6pm Tue–Sat) ■ Adm

An extensive collection of worldwide puppet traditions *(see pp68–9)*.

8 Museo di Zoologia P Doderlein
MAP P6 ■ Via Archirafi 16 ■ 091 23891819 ■ Open 10am–1pm Tue–Sat, 5–8pm Sun ■ Adm

Learn about Sicily's diverse animals and evolution through an array of preserved specimens displayed here.

9 Cappuccini Catacombs
MAP N2 ■ Via Cappuccini 1 ■ Open 9am–1pm, 3–6pm daily (closed Oct–Mar & Sun pm) ■ Adm

Burial site of Palermo's upper classes (1599–1881). Not suitable for children.

10 Mondello
MAP D2

This fishing village *(see p60)* became a trendy resort in the 19th century.

Places to Shop

1 Via della Libertà
MAP J1

Upscale Italian chains line the street between the Teatro Politeama and Piazza Francesco Crispi: try Longho (No. 42) for concept furnishings, Louis Vuitton (No. 7) for leather goods, and Max Mara (No. 16/a) for luxury women's fashion and accessories.

2 Via Enrico Parisi
MAP J1

For menswear, step just off Via della Libertà to find high fashion at Uomo Store (No. 21/c) and chic boutiques such as Visiona Uomo (No. 11 Via Enrico Parisi). Afterwards, stop in at the equally chic Baretto, round the corner on Via XX Settembre 43, for an *aperitivo*.

3 Ceramiche De Simone
MAP L3 ■ Via Cavour 38

The de Simone family has been producing hand-painted ceramics for generations, with designs of jolly Sicilian farmers as well as fishermen.

4 La Coppola Storta
MAP L3 ■ Via Bara all'Olivella 103

The traditional Sicilian cap has been given a new lease of life thanks to this innovative store. All sorts of hats are available.

5 Rinascente
MAP M4 ■ Via Roma 289

Italy's most upmarket department store has an outlet on this shopping street. There's a selection of Italian *haute couture* and accessories, and a good houseware department.

6 Enoteca Picone
MAP J1 ■ Via Marconi 36

As well as over 7,000 different beverages, you'll find olive oil and cheeses here *[see p83]*.

Shopping in Palermo's markets

7 Markets

Some of the best shopping in Palermo happens at the three daily food markets *(see p83)*. They are well worth visiting even if you don't intend to buy anything.

8 Punto Pizzo Free, L'Emporio
MAP M4 ■ Via Vittorio Emanuele 172

The traditional products sold here *(see p83)* come from various boutiques around the city, the owners of which have refused to pay the *pizzo*, or Mafia protection money.

Sicilian caps for sale at La Coppola Storta

9 Vincenzo Argento
MAP L5 ■ Via Vittorio Emanuele 445

For four generations the Argento family has been practising the art of puppetry. They make traditional puppets in the Palermitan style *(see p68)* for sale and to use in rousing shows in their nearby theatre *(see p69)*.

10 Franco Bertolino
MAP K5 ■ Via Simone di Bologna 15, behind the Cathedral

Hand-painted *carrettini*, traditional Sicilian miniature carts, are sold here along with beautifully crafted papier-mâché figures and fruit.

See map on pp90–91

Nights Out

Impressive Teatro Massimo

① Teatro Massimo
MAP K3 ▪ Piazza Verdi ▪ Guided tours ▪ www.teatromassimo.it

Palermo's historic theatre reopened in 1997 after a major restoration effort. It stages lyrical opera, ballet and symphonic concerts.

② Teatro di Verdura
MAP D2 ▪ Viale del Fante 70

Opera, ballet, concerts and plays are presented in summer in this outdoor theatre in the garden of the former villa of the Prince of Castelnuovo.

③ Teatro Politeama Garibaldi
MAP K2 ▪ Via Turati 2 ▪ 091 6072524

This Neo-Classical theatre was opened in 1874. The season offers symphonic concerts and ballet.

④ Teatro Biondo Stabile
MAP L4 ▪ Via Roma 258 ▪ 091 7434341

The Biondo brothers founded this centre for experimental theatre.

⑤ Santa Maria dello Spasimo
MAP P5 ▪ Via dello Spasimo 10 ▪ 091 6166490 ▪ Open 8am–8pm daily ▪ Adm

A bombed-out church that acts as a performance venue and art gallery, Santa Maria dello Spasimo *(see p70)* has a full programme of films and concerts (classical, contemporary, jazz), romantically staged in the roofless nave and garden space.

⑥ Associazione Culturale Palab
MAP K6 ▪ Via Fondaco Palazzo Reale 5 ▪ 320 9040746

A combination of cultural centre, theatre, music and comedy club, cinema, cocktail bar, pizzeria and restaurant, this place is always bustling with activity.

⑦ Via dei Chiavettieri
MAP M4

This pedestrian street is buzzing well into the early hours of the morning. It is lined with clubs and pubs, many with outside tables and live music.

⑧ Teatro Co-Op Agricantus
MAP J1 ▪ Via Nicolò Garzilli 89 ▪ 091 309636 ▪ www.agricantus.org

Agricantus is a performing arts co-op staging high-quality theatre and music, particularly for children.

⑨ Piazza Olivella
MAP L3

At night the piazza between Teatro Massimo and Via Cavour fills up with university students hanging out in the many bars lining the square.

⑩ La Cuba
MAP N2 ▪ Villa Sperlinga, Via Francesco Scaduto 12 ▪ 091 300846

This multipurpose venue in the beautiful Villa Sperlinga, a little way out of central Palermo, draws a smart crowd by offering good food, drinks and a programme of live music and DJs.

Places to Eat

1 Cin Cin
MAP K1 ▪ Via Manin 22 ▪ 091 6124095 ▪ Closed Sun ▪ €€

Tucked away on a side street, Chef Vincenzo creatively melds traditional Sicilian cuisine with a touch of the American South in this restaurant.

2 Piccolo Napoli
MAP K2 ▪ Piazzetta Mulino a Vento 4 ▪ 328 6044380 ▪ Closed Sun ▪ €€

Try the pasta with lobster or any fish dish at this family-run trattoria *(see p78)* in the little market square behind the Teatro Politeama Garibaldi.

3 Osteria Mercede
MAP K3 ▪ Via Sammartino 1 ▪ 091 332243 ▪ Closed Mon & Tue lunch ▪ €

Near Teatro Massimo, this small place serves delectable fish dishes that marry tradition and innovation. The chalkboard menu changes daily according to the catch.

Airy interior of Antica Focacceria

4 Antica Focacceria
MAP M4 ▪ Via A Paternostro 58 (Piazza S Francesco) ▪ 091 320264 ▪ Closed mid-Jan ▪ €

Feast on Palermitan fast food and main courses such as sandwiches, panelle *(see p77)* and foccacia under the façade of San Francesco.

PRICE CATEGORIES

For a three-course meal for one with half a bottle of wine (or equivalent meal), taxes and extra charges.

€ under €35   €€ €35–€70   €€€ over €70

5 Lilla e Totuccio
MAP L3 ▪ Via Bara all'Olivella 91 ▪ 320 292 6255 ▪ €

This street-food spot frequented by young *Palermitani* offers a buffet of simple, tasty food, including pasta dishes. Even with wine, it's a bargain.

6 Ferro di Cavallo
MAP L4 ▪ Via Venezia 20 ▪ 091 331835 ▪ Closed Sun ▪ €

Join the locals at this casual trattoria not far from the Quattro Canti for traditional fare and great people-watching opportunites.

7 Freschette
MAP L4 ▪ Via Quintino Sella 17 ▪ 393 2430440 ▪ €

An organic, vegetarian café and market with plenty of local produce for sale and on the menu.

8 Zia Pina
MAP M4 ▪ Via Cassari 69 ▪ 331 981 4546 ▪ €

There may be brusque service and shabby decor at Zia Pina, but it serves arguably the best seafood in town, and at a bargain price.

9 Osteria dei Vespri
MAP M5 ▪ Piazza Croce dei Vespri 6 ▪ 091 6171631 ▪ Closed Sun ▪ €€€

A chic spot in a *palazzo* famous for being featured in Luchino Visconti's film *The Leopard*.

10 Bye Bye Blues
MAP D2 ▪ Via del Garofolo 23, Mondello ▪ 091 6841415 ▪ Closed Mon ▪ €€€

Excellent Sicilian ingredients are chosen for inventive dishes at this Michelin-starred spot.

See map on pp90–91 ←

TOP 10 Northwest Sicily

Much of this area presents unique opportunities to wander through fishing villages, watch shepherds at work and witness a way of life that has survived for centuries. The coast and offshore islands are pristine, while the mountainous interior has some of the harshest terrain in Sicily. Farmers still use mules in their fields, though younger generations are developing vineyards to produce high-quality Sicilian wines.

Blue waters and rocky cliffs of the Egadi Islands

NORTHWEST SICILY

Tyrrhenian Sea

Capo San Vito

San Vito lo Capo ① ⑨ ⑤ ①

Aeroporto Falcone-Borsellino

Terrasini

Golfo di Cófano

Castelluzzo

⑥ Lo Zingaro

④

Golfo di Bonagia

⑧ Custonaci

Castellammare del Golfo

② ⑤ Erice

⑥ ④ Valderice

⑤ Scopello   Balestrate

Partinico

Marettimo 30 km (18 miles)

Isola di Levanzo

② ④ ⑧ ③ ⑦ Trapani ①

Levanzo

A29

S113

Lago Poma

② Egadi Islands

Favignana

④ ⑥

Isola Favignana

⑩ ⑩ Paceco

A29dir

Fulgatore

Segesta ③

⑥ Alcamo

Aeroporto di Trapani-Birgi

Rilievo

⑦

Ummari

⑧

Calatafimi

Camporeale

Isole dello Stagnone

S115

Motya ⑨

Vita

Val di Mázara

Tabaccaro

Salemi

Gibellina Vecchia

Marsala ⑩

① ⑥

⑨

Strasatti

Mázaro

Lago della Trinità

Santa Ninfa

Partanna ①

② ②

Lago Garci

⑦ Pantelleria 100 km (62 miles)

Pizzolato

E931

③ ⑧ Castelvetrano

Montevago ⑦

Santa Margherita di Belice

④

A29

Campobello di Mazara

Belice

S115

Sambuca di Sicilia

Mazara del Vallo

⑤

⑦ ③

Menfi

S115

⑤

Porto Palo ⑩

0 kilometres   15

0 miles   15

Selinunte

1 Trapani
MAP B2

A busy port since Spanish rule, Trapani is still a bustling place. The modern town has grown but the lively historic centre is on the tiny peninsula – the area covers less than 2.5 sq km. The main streets are lined with a mix of Baroque buildings, shops and cafés. Via Torrearsa leads from the port to the market square with its lovely loggia, and the Corso leads to the tip of the peninsula, with glimpses of everyday Sicilian life in the side streets.

2 Egadi Islands
MAP A3 ■ **Hydrofoil and ferry: Trapani**

Levanzo, Favignana and Marettimo can be reached from Trapani in as little as 20 minutes by hydrofoil and are great for relaxing on a summer's day, as there is pretty much nothing here except for the sea. They are most famous for the *mattanza*, the Arabic tuna-fishing ritual that is still practised here in spring. Favignana is dotted with tufa quarries that give the island a pockmarked look; the caves of Levanzo's interior have Paleolithic and Neolithic paintings, and the swimming is good on all three islands. Marettimo, the furthest from the mainland (an hour from Trapani), is known for its extraordinarily clear waters.

Interior of Monreale Cathedral

3 Monreale

On this royal hill *(mons reale)* Sicily's Norman king, William II, built the mosaic-encrusted monastery and cathedral *(see pp14–15)* that proved to be the last and most splendid of the island's Norman monuments.

4 Erice
MAP B2 ■ **www.funiviaerice.it**

On top of a cliff above Trapani, ancient Eryx was known for its temple to Venus Erycina, so large that it served as a beacon to sailors at sea. The temple was replaced with a castle in the Middle Ages, and the village still has a medieval look. The main industry here is tourism. Local artisans make good ceramics and rugs, and the views are spectacular.

5 Selinunte

The ruins of this Greek city *(see pp36–9)*, including temples, walls, marketplace and homes, stand majestically backed by the sea – silent reminders of the glory of the once great city.

Reserva Naturale dello Zingaro

6 Lo Zingaro
MAP B2

Sicily's first nature reserve was instituted in 1980 to protect 7 km (4 miles) of rocky coastline on the Tyrrhenian Sea between Scopello and San Vito lo Capo. Marked trails of various levels of difficulty traverse the steep interior, or creep along the cliff above the sea, occasionally forking down to small coves with pebble beaches. The reserve protects flora and fauna such as wild orchids, limonium, wild carnations, dwarf palms, iris, once-widespread ilex and cork-oak forests, lichens and ferns, Bonelli's eagles, Sicilian warblers, peregrine falcons, owls, porcupines and foxes.

7 Pantelleria
MAP A6 ■ Hydrofoils: Liberty Lines; 092 3022022 ■ Flights: Palermo and Trapani

This tiny volcanic island is actually closer to Africa than Italy. The architecture reflects Arabic influences and the island is dotted with *dammusi* – low, whitewashed, domed houses. Pantelleria is renowned for its top-quality caper production and the thick and sweet *passito* wine, made from the native Zibibbo grape, which grows well despite the ever-present *scirocco* winds that blow from the sea.

8 Segesta
MAP C3 ■ 4 km (2 miles) from Calatafimi ■ Open Mar & Oct: 9am–6:30pm daily (Apr–Sep: to 7:30pm daily; Nov–Feb: to 5pm daily) ■ Adm

Tucked between the green hills and rugged mountains west of Calatafimi, Segesta *(see p44)* has the most romantic ruins in Sicily. The temple was built in perfect, solid Doric proportions (c 420 BC) and stands isolated on a gentle slope, turning pink in the sunset. Missing *cella*, ungrooved columns and studs around the stylobate hint that it was unfinished. The theatre, high up on Monte Barbaro, is still in use.

MARSALA WINE

When John Woodhouse shipped local wine to Liverpool in the 18th century, conserving it with extra alcohol, he "discovered" Marsala. The product took off and along with Englishmen Ingham and Whitaker and Italian Florio, they began a business fortifying local wine. In the 20th century, industrial versions were considered cooking wine but recent products are high quality.

9 Motya

MAP B3 ▪ Museo Whitaker: open Apr–Oct: 9:30am–6:30pm daily; Nov–Mar: 9am–3pm daily ▪ Adm

This archaeological park occupies an entire island in Lo Stagnone, the lagoon north of Marsala, where the 8th-century BC Phoenician and later Carthaginian city of Motya (Mozia in Italian) thrived. Dionysus I of Syracuse destroyed it in 398 BC, leaving it in ruins. The large archaeological collections of the Museo Whitaker (former home of the English Marsala-producing family) include the striking Greek marble statue of a youth in a diaphanous pleated tunic (c 440 BC).

Greek statue, Motya

10 Marsala

MAP B3 ▪ Museo Archeologico Baglio Anselmi: Lungomare Boéo; open 9am–6:30pm Tue–Sat (to 1:30pm Sun); adm

This sunbaked seaside town was named by the Arabs: Marsa Allah (the port of God). It is known as the landing point for Garibaldi's Redshirts (see p43) and for the wine named after it. The Marsala wine trade was born in the 18th century. The Baglio Anselmi is an archaeological museum that houses the treasures of Marsala's Punic past.

Roman theatre, Segesta

A DAY EXPLORING TRAPANI

Torre di Ligny
Trapani Market
Piazza Mercato del Pesce
Taverna Paradiso
Ceramiche Perrone
San Lorenzo Cathedral
Corso Vittorio Emanuele
Via Torrearsa
Erice 13 km (8 miles)
Egadi Islands 38 km (23 miles)
Church of Sant'Agostino

▶ MORNING

Start off your day with a visit to the colourful **Trapani Market**, which is held at the port, at Torre di Ligny. Well-stocked vendors are happy to offer tasters of cheeses, olives and tuna to potential customers. This is a great place to pick out a few things for a picnic. Next, walk up Corso Vittorio Emanuele and take a look at the handcrafted ceramic pieces at **Ceramiche Perrone** (see p104).

Going down Corso Vittorio Emanuele, crane your neck to see the green majolica domes of San Lorenzo Cathedral, before turning off for Il Tonno in Piazza, in Piazza Mercato del Pesce, to top up your picnic provisions. When Corso Vittorio Emanuele runs into **Via Torrearsa** (see p99), walk a few hundred metres to the right to visit the beautiful **Church of Sant'Agostino** (Via Sant'Agostino), which has a 14th-century rose window, before passing through the arch and back onto Via Torrearsa. Stop at the end of the peninsula to enjoy your picnic lunch and the sea views.

AFTERNOON

Either spend the afternoon shopping in Trapani, or head up to **Erice** (see p99) for its views. You can also take the hydrofoil to the **Egadi Islands** (see p99).

Make it back to Trapani in time for the sunset to take part in the local *passeggiata*, then enjoy a fish dinner at **Taverna Paradiso** (see p105). Order some *gelato* or the Sicilan *cassata* for dessert.

See map on pp98–9 ←

The Best of the Rest

The exquisite interior of the Baroque Villa Palagonia, Bagheria

1 Bagheria
MAP D2

This village east of Palermo is now rather developed, but you can still see the elaborate Baroque villas built by Palermo's nobility, when it was all citrus groves and orchards.

2 Cretto di Burri
MAP C3

Italian painter and sculptor Alberto Burri created this enormous outdoor cement sculpture in 1984. It is a sombre monument to the lives lost in Gibellina in the 1968 earthquake.

3 Castelvetrano
MAP B3

The "City of Olives and Temples", known for its olive oil production, owes the Arabs its urban plan and its maze of piazzas. The bronze *Ephebus* (c 470 BC) is in the Museo Civico.

4 Mazara del Vallo
MAP B3

This fishing port is home to the lovely Hellenic bronze statue of the *Satiro Danzante* ("dancing satyr"), found on the seabed by fishermen in 1997.

5 Cusa Quarries
MAP B3 ▪ Near Campobello di Mazara

Set amid olive trees, this natural quarry for Selinunte has tufa blocks and half-cut columns, which had to be hauled 9km (6 miles) to the city.

6 Alcamo
MAP C2

This village has a 14th-century castle of the Spanish Counts of Modica, who once ruled much of the region. It is best known for Bianco d'Alcamo, a white wine with DOC protection.

7 Marinella di Selinunte
MAP C4

A fishing village with a great morning market and a small historic centre of fishermen's homes at the port. The boardwalk is lined with restaurants, bars and bathing establishments.

8 Solunto
MAP D2

The Greek village of Solus was built on top of a Carthaginian settlement, high above the sea. Lacking natural springs, it developed a clever way to conserve water. Among the ruins are cisterns, channels and pools.

9 San Vito lo Capo
MAP B2

On this dramatic promontory is a resort with a long sandy beach and a busy promenade in summer.

10 Saline, Saltpans
MAP B2 ▪ Museo del Sale: Via Chiusa, Nubia, Paceco; open 9:30am–7pm daily; adm

Exceptional sea salt is produced here using 16th-century windmills. Visit the Museo del Sale in Paceco *(see p66)*.

Landscape Features

① Rolling Hillsides
MAP C3

The rolling hills of the Belice valley are planted with wheat – green in winter, gold in summer and burned black after the harvest – bordered by grapevines and olive groves.

② Poggioreale Hill
MAP C3

On the road from the ruins of Poggioreale to the new town, a single wheat-covered hill rises up, topped with a lone wild pear tree.

③ Rugged Mountains
MAP C3

The rugged hills around Segesta, Calatafimi and Alcamo look dry and barren, but resourceful Sicilians plant them with sturdy vines, cultivating the hills as high as possible.

④ Quarries
MAP B2

The rocky mountains between Trapani, San Vito lo Capo and Castellamare del Golfo are rich in marble, but are slowly being destroyed by industrial quarries extracting the stone.

⑤ Beaches

Long sandy beaches line the western coast of Sicily, reaching up to the huge stretch of sand at San Vito lo Capo. Pebble beaches are found to the northwest, on the coast of the Golfo di Castellammare.

Clear waters at San Vito lo Capo

⑥ Faraglione
MAP C2

The rock towers at Scopello Tonnara jut out of the water and are circled by seagulls who nest in rock crevices.

⑦ Belice Valley

Near its mouth the wide, fertile Belice valley is long, low, flat and very good for farming; it's covered with a patchwork quilt of vineyards, olive groves, melon vines and citrus fruit trees. It is traversed by a typical Sicilian highway, raised on tall stilts.

Farmed fields on the hillsides, Belice

⑧ Promontories
MAP B2

The enormous rocky headlands rising up by the sea include Monte San Giuliano (with Erice on top), Monte Cofano (with spectacular bays and a great view of Erice), and Monte Monaco at San Vito lo Capo.

⑨ Plain

The mountains of the interior flatten as they near the sea towards Mazara, Marsala and up to Trapani on the northwest coast. The low, sunbaked ground is fertile territory for grapes, olives and the saltpans.

⑩ Erosion

The Romans deforested Sicily to plant wheat. The result is almost treeless earth, mostly parched and prone to drastic run-off during rains.

See map on pp98–9 ←

Traditional Shops

Airy interior of the Cantine Pellegrino

1 Cantine Pellegrino, Marsala

MAP B3 ▪ Via del Fante 39 ▪ www.carlopellegrino.it

This established Marsala family winery offers tastings and tours (in various languages) of the cellars.

2 Pasticceria Artigianale Grammatico Maria, Erice

MAP B2 ▪ Via Vittorio Emanuele 14

A specialist sweet shop (see p80), this place offers a wide range of treats made according to recipes collected over the centuries by the sisters of Erice's San Carlo monastery.

3 Ceramiche Perrone, Trapani

MAP B2 ▪ Corso Vittorio Emanuele 102

In addition to ceramic plates, this family-run business also produces traditional figurines for nativity scenes, modelled on Sicilian peasants, and miniature terracotta replicas of traditional foods.

4 La Casa del Tonno, Favignana

MAP B2 ▪ Via Roma 12 ▪ www.iltonno.com

The name, the House of Tuna, says it all. In central Favignana, the location of the ancient tuna-fishing method called the *mattanza* (see p53), try this shop for canned tuna in oil and *bottarga* (dried tuna egg).

5 Altieri 1882, Erice

MAP B2 ▪ Via Cordici 10

Since 1882, Altieri (see p82) has been producing their original pieces in gold, coral and ceramic.

6 Cantine Florio, Marsala

MAP B3 ▪ Via Vincenzo Florio 1 ▪ www.duca.it/florio

Inside the Florio wine cellars is a store and a wine museum with a selection of antique tools used for winemaking.

7 Taberna Gustus, Trapani

MAP B2 ▪ Via Libertà 9

A food and wine shop with a great selection of local vintages, sparkling wines, liqueurs, oils and confectionery, as well as handmade artisanal speciality items.

8 La Bottega del Pane Rizzo, Castelvetrano

MAP B3 ▪ Via Garibaldi 85

Master baker Tommaso Rizzo uses local ingredients, natural yeast and a wood-burning oven to make the traditional *pane nero di Castelvetrano*, a tasty dark-brown bread. There are also the delicious *biscotti piccanti*, biscuits made with black pepper and anise. Other biscuits incorporate honey, sesame seeds and figs.

9 A Maidda, San Vito lo Capo

MAP B2 ▪ Via Regina Margherita 52

A nice selection of Sicilian treats and wines – but they don't come cheap.

10 Museo del Sale, Paceco

The museum store (see p102) sells boxes of traditionally produced sea salt. The salt's rich flavour as well as its saltiness can vary, depending on the climatic conditions. The fine grain of the stone-ground salt also adds a pleasant texture to foods.

Places to Eat

1 Pocho, San Vito lo Capo

MAP B2 ▪ Località Isulidda,
Makari ▪ 092 3972525 ▪ Closed
Oct–Easter ▪ €€

Dine in an eclectic dining room *(see
p78)* with puppets hanging in the corners or on the breezy terrace looking
down at Monte Cofano and the bay.

2 Taverna Paradiso, Trapani

MAP B2 ▪ Lungomare Dante Alighieri
22 ▪ 092 322303 ▪ Closed Thu am ▪ €€

Locally caught fish prepared simply
and with skill. Congenial service.

A platter of seafood from Trapani

3 La Pineta, Selinunte

MAP B4 ▪ Via Punta Cantone
▪ 092 446820 ▪ €

Expertly prepared fresh fish served
on the beach under torchlight.

4 Cantina Siciliana, Trapani

MAP B2 ▪ Via Giudecca 36 ▪ 092
328673 ▪ €

Chef Pino Maggiore offers traditional
fare at this restaurant *(see
p79)*, such as couscous
and almond pesto.

5 Ristorante La Terrazza, Scopello

MAP C2 ▪ Via Marco
Polo 5 ▪ 092 4534843
▪ €€

Fresh fish, caught for the
restaurant, and fine views.

PRICE CATEGORIES

For a three-course meal for one with half a
bottle of wine (or equivalent meal), taxes
and extra charges.

€ under €35   €€ €35–€70   €€€ over €70

6 La Bettola, Favignana

MAP A3 ▪ Via Nicotera 47
▪ 092 3921988 ▪ Closed Mon ▪ €

The menu includes the catch of the
day and a few vegetable dishes. A
good place to eat when the tuna
are in season.

7 Agriturismo Vultaggio, Guarrato, near Trapani

MAP B2 ▪ Contrada Misiliscemi
Guarrato ▪ 092 3864261 ▪ €€

Enjoy traditional Sicilian food at this
agritourism farm that produces its
own wine, oil and citrus fruits.

8 Le Vele, Trapani

MAP B2 ▪ Via Serisso 18
▪ 347 4219772 ▪ €

Elegant without being extravagant,
Le Vele offers great pizzas. While
they also serve fish cooked in
the traditional Trapani style, their
speciality is *patate alla vastasa*,
which is spicy potatoes with onion
and cheese.

9 Bricco & Bacco, Monreale

MAP C2 ▪ Via Benedetto d'Acquisto
13 ▪ 091 6417773 ▪ €€

The fare is inspired by the hearty
dishes of Sicily's interior. Look for
antipasti, meat (including *trippa*,
or tripe) and vegetable sides.

10 Le 4 Stagioni, Menfi

MAP C3 ▪ Via delle
Margherite 15
▪ 092 578447 ▪ €€

This unpretentious
hotel restaurant
serves top-quality
Sicilian fish specialities
and pasta dishes.

**A well-presented dish
at Le 4 Stagioni**

See map on pp98–9 ←

TOP 10 Northeast Sicily

The northeast of Sicily is dominated by Mount Etna, although the region also consists of three mountain ranges, a group of islands with another active volcano, and two of Sicily's largest cities. Parts of this area have been hit by wars, earthquakes, tidal waves and lava flows, but the land and the people return from each ordeal more steadfast. Perhaps that is why feast days of the patron saints are celebrated with so much fervour. High in the Nebrodi and Madonie mountains, it seems like nothing has changed for eons – the same castles that guarded the royal paths of the interior now keep watch over the modern *autostrada*.

Crater on Vulcano Island

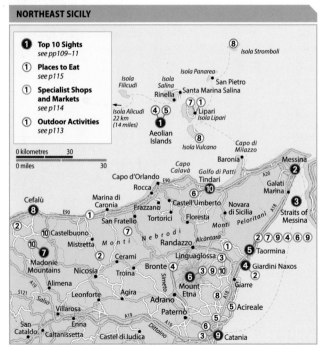

NORTHEAST SICILY

1 Top 10 Sights
see pp109–11

1 Places to Eat
see p115

1 Specialist Shops and Markets
see p114

1 Outdoor Activities
see p113

0 kilometres 30
0 miles 30

Previous pages Catania's Duomo and the Fountain of the Elephant

1 Aeolian Islands

These islands *(see pp16–17)* were declared a World Heritage Site by UNESCO in recognition of the ongoing evolution of the volcanic forms that create their spectacular scenery. The islands remain an important study area for vulcanologists.

2 Messina
MAP H2

Founded by colonists from Messenia, Greece, the city grew up around the harbour. In 1908, Messina was levelled by an earthquake and tidal wave, though parts of the older city survived, including the Norman Duomo with its original portals and sculpture, a 15th-century fountain in the Piazza Duomo and a clock tower whose mechanized figures perform at noon. The Santissima Annunziata dei Catalani and the Museo Regionale, with works by Messina *(see p56)* and Caravaggio *(see p50)*, also survived.

3 Straits of Messina
MAP H2

The narrow strait between Messina and Reggio di Calabria was said to be guarded by Scylla and Charybdis, mythical sea creatures who led sailors astray. A proposed suspension bridge linking Sicily and mainland Italy has been under debate for more than 30 years. Some Sicilians believe a link to the mainland would bring much-needed economic development, others fear a loss of their autonomy.

4 Giardini Naxos
MAP H3 ■ Site and museum: open 9am–6:30pm daily ■ Adm

Naxos was founded in 734 BC, and became the first Greek settlement in Sicily. It was the setting off point for messengers taking news to Greece. The ruins, defensive walls and parts of a temple are enclosed in a park. A small museum houses local finds.

San Giuseppe church, Taormina

5 Taormina

Sicily's first true holiday resort, Taormina *(see pp18–19)* has been drawing visitors for centuries, all of whom fall in love with the sparkling, colourful beauty of the area.

6 Mount Etna

Europe's largest active volcano *(see pp20–21)* dominates Sicily – from much of the island it is rarely out of sight and never out of mind.

Mount Etna in the distance

Sandy beach at Cefalù

7 Madonie Mountains
MAP E3

The Madonie range, featuring Sicily's highest peaks after Mount Etna, extends from Cefalù inland and is protected by the Parco Naturale Regionale delle Madonie. The park, which encompasses spectacular countryside, includes tiny villages, forests of beech, chestnuts, cork oaks, poplars and fir. The remote villages that once provided refuge to bandits on the run are now good starting points for outdoor activities (see pp64–5), such as hikes, horse riding, cycling and skiing.

View over the Madonie Mountains

8 Cefalù
MAP E2

This small fishing town is now a resort and must-visit area thanks to its picturesque sandy beaches and impressive Cathedral (see p47). Its location on a strip of land between the sea and a huge promontory looming above is also a draw. Cefalù was founded in the 4th century BC but destroyed by the Norman Count Roger in 1063. It only regained prominence thanks to his son, Roger II, who endowed the village with a bishopric and an imposing church decorated with exceptional Byzantine mosaics. The town has managed to retain its medieval character despite the arrival of modern holiday resorts. The resorts lie to either side of Cefalù because the town itself has closed its doors to the sea. It has fortified itself against storms by building tall protective stone walls, and focuses its attention inland instead.

FROM ICE TO ICE CREAM

Greeks and Romans used Mount Etna's snow to chill their wine, and the Arabs used it to make cold, sweet drinks. Sicilians were used to mixing ice, sugar and natural flavours (cinnamon, lemon, jasmine) to make granita and sorbet but by the 1700s they had perfected the craft of ice-cream-making, adding chocolate brought by the Spanish from the New World. Sicilian gelato (see p76) is now famous the world over.

A MORNING WALK AROUND CEFALÙ

9 Catania
MAP G4

After a huge earthquake in 1693, the city was rebuilt in a unique Baroque style. The most important monuments are around the Piazza Duomo, including the Duomo itself.

Archaeological park, Tindari

10 Tindari
MAP G2

The large ruins of ancient Tyndaris, first Greek and then Roman, lie either side of the Decumanus Maximus, the main street. Homes show mosaic floors, drainage and heating systems. A restored basilica spans the street where it marked the entrance into the public area. The theatre, built by the Greeks, modified by the Romans and still in use, has views out to sea. A small museum houses finds from the site including a colossal head of Augustus. Nearby is the sanctuary of the Black Madonna.

Start your walk at Piazza Garibaldi, beginning at Corso Ruggero, where the Church of Santa Maria della Catena (see p92) is built on top of the 4th-century BC town walls. Down the Corso, on the left at the corner of Via Amendola is one of the only extant parts of Norman Cefalù, besides the cathedral, the *palazzo* Osterio Magno. Pass the flower-filled *piazzetta* in front of the Chiesa del Purgatorio on your way to Piazza del Duomo, which opens up to the right. Inside the **Cathedral** (see p47) admire the mosaics, and view the outside of the apse around the back. Sit out in the piazza at **Bar Duomo** (*Piazza del Duomo 24*) with a cappuccino and enjoy the cathedral façade and the church bells marking the hour.

Continue down the Corso to the end, take a left onto Via Bordonaro and a right into Piazza Crispi with views of the Greek walls later absorbed by Spanish fortifications. Follow Via Bordonaro down to Piazza Marina with the small port below. Off to the left, down the Via Vittorio Emanuele, a staircase leads to the *lavatoio* (washbasins), the sole remnant of Arab domination.

Before lunch, wander around the "real" Cefalù, where fishermen repair boats and women pause from their laundry to chat.

Have lunch in the garden at **Il Normanno** (*Via Vanni 9, near Corso Ruggero*) or get some picnic supplies from Alimentari e Salumeria Gatta Gaetano (*Corso Ruggero 152*).

See map on p108 ←

Mount Etna Eruptions

1 693 BC
This massive volcanic eruption destroyed the Greek settlement at Katane (ancient Catania).

2 396 BC
Lava flows from this eruption reached the Ionian Sea, preventing the Carthaginian Himilco from landing and consequently stopping him from marching on Syracuse.

3 1169, 1329 and 1381
The eruptions in these three years sent lava spilling out all the way to the sea. The first caused lava to reach Aci Castello; the last flowed all the way to Catania, pouring into the sea at Ognina and covering the Portus Ulixis, which was mentioned by Virgil in the epic poem *The Aeneid*.

4 1669
The worst eruption in modern times was preceded by three days of earthquakes. On the third day, a huge crevice 14 km (8.5 miles) long stretched to Nicolosi and disgorged ash, rocks and lava. The eruption lasted four months, destroying towns and leaving 27,000 people homeless.

5 1886
Lava flows from this eruption once again threatened the village of Nicolosi, but the veil of St Agatha was carried in a procession and the lava miraculously stopped. It was not the first time that St Agatha had purportedly halted a lava flow.

6 1911
Two major eruptions on the north side created a 5-km- (3-mile-) long crevice and 170 craters. The crevice opened up again in 1923.

7 1928
A huge eruption destroyed the town of Mascali, a significant amount of cultivated land and several buildings. This was the only occasion during the 20th century when a town had been destroyed.

8 1979
An explosion killed nine tourists who were on the edge of the main crater, then poured lava into the Valle del Bove, nearly reaching Fornazzo.

9 1991–3
Lava flowed down the Valle del Bove towards Zafferana Etnea; the authorities tried to divert the flow with explosives and by dropping concrete blocks from helicopters. The lava finally stopped just 1 km (half a mile) from the village.

10 2001–2
The most complex eruption in 300 years took place in 2001, when Etna disgorged ash and lava from six openings on the north and southeast sides, destroying the Etna Sud cable-car station. During the 2002 eruption visitors' centres and hotels were ruined, and Catania airport closed.

Plume of smoke from Mount Etna

Outdoor Activities

Alcàntara River and Gorge

① Alcàntara Gorge
The Alcàntara River runs at the bottom of a 20-m- (65-ft-) deep basalt gorge. From the car park, with waders for hire, walk or take the lift to the bottom. You can hike between the narrow walls and over waterfalls.

② Horse Riding, Madonie
Agriturismo Casalvecchio Geraci: Geraci Siculo; 334 1362149 ■ Sicily on Horseback: Collesano; 347 8125470
The trails of the Madonie can be used by horse riders too. There are various riding stables, some of which are attached to good restaurants.

③ Skiing, Mount Etna
Etna Sud Ski School: 347 6551793 ■ Etna Nord Ski School & Etna Nord Snowboarding: 347 6551793; www.scuolaitaliana scietna.it
There are about 10 ski runs on Etna. Lift tickets and equipment hire are available.

④ Swimming, Aeolian Islands
Good swimming abounds in the Aeolians – the water is clear and rich in marine life.

⑤ Boating, Aeolian Islands
The best way to visit hidden coves and grottoes, and the only way to get from island to island, is by boat. A wide selection of organized tours dock on the seven islands. Boat hire is also available.

⑥ Walking, Tindari
Below the promontory, from Capo Tindari towards Oliveri and Falcone, the Tindari-Oliveri reserve has quiet walks by sand formations and lakes with blue-green water.

⑦ Hiking, Nebrodi
The Nebrodi Mountain Park offers pastureland, yew and beech woods, birds of prey, a wetlands habitat for migratory birds, and wild horses. There are 21 villages, where artisans produce goods and food. There are marked trails for hiking.

⑧ Hiking, Aeolian Islands
Hike up the slopes to Vulcano's crater following the signs *"al cratere"*. Or take a guide from the hydrofoil dock up the active volcano Stromboli.

Hiking a trail on Mount Etna

⑨ Hiking, Mount Etna
Gruppo Guide Alpine Etna Sud: 095 7914755; www.etnaguide. eu ■ Gruppo Guide Alpine Etna Nord: 095 7774502; www.guidetnanord.com
Ascend to the main crater or hike the slopes accompanied by a guide.

⑩ Hiking, Madonie
Italian Alpine Club: 092 2057231 ■ www.cai.it
The Madonie mountains have marked trails graded for difficulty; some are suitable for travellers with specific requirements. The Italian Alpine Club organizes guided tours.

See map on p108

Specialist Shops and Markets

Ceramics, Santo Stefano di Camastra

1 Ceramics, Santo Stefano di Camastra
MAP H2

Shops selling Santo Stefano's famous orange-and-yellow ceramics abound.

2 'A Putia, Giardini-Naxos
MAP H3 ▪ Via Umberto I 456 and Lungomare IV Novembre 249

A vast array of delicious Sicilian products, including wine, cheese, honey, pistachios and preserves. There is also a restaurant.

3 Via Etnea, Catania
MAP G4

Big-name Italian stores such as Max Mara, Benetton, Rinascente as well as pastry shops and cafés. Emporio Armani and designer shops continue on the Corso Italia.

4 Le Colonne, Taormina
MAP H3 ▪ Corso Umberto 164

The proprietor of this jewellery store *(see p82)* in Taormina creates pieces from old stones, inspired by historical motifs; or you can create your own design.

5 Cantine Privitera, Gravina di Catania
MAP G4 ▪ Via Nino Martoglio 33

Located just above Catania, this shop sells honey, wine, mead, honey vinegar, propolis and soaps.

6 Ceramiche dell'Artigianato Siciliano di Managò, Taormina
MAP H3 ▪ Piazza San Domenico 1/2

Signor Managò's Sicilian ceramics include designs from Caltagirone and Santo Stefano di Camastra.

7 Fratelli Laise, Lipari
MAP G1 ▪ Via Vittorio Emanuele 188

This store's booty of Aeolian goods includes capers, sundried tomatoes, honey, oregano and wine.

8 Markets
In villages on the slopes of Mount Etna, such as Fleri, farmers sell their produce from their trucks.

9 La Torinese, Taormina
MAP H3 ▪ Corso Umberto 59

Since 1936, La Torinese has sold quality wines and liqueurs, tuna roe, salami, honey and olive oil.

10 Mount Etna Souvenirs
MAP G3

The best in lava kitsch can be found at the base of Etna Sud or Etna Nord. Ashtrays, mini statues and animal figures have been moulded from molten lava and dipped in glitter.

Souvenirs made from lava

Places to Eat

1 Ristorante Nenzyna, Lipari

MAP G1 ▪ Via Roma 4 ▪ 090 9811660 ▪ Closed Nov–Easter ▪ €

A tiny trattoria where the owner has been preparing fresh fish and other favourites for more than 40 years.

2 Osteria Nero d'Avola, Taormina

MAP H3 ▪ Piazza San Domenico 2b ▪ 347 8182161 ▪ Closed Mon ▪ €€

Considered an ambassador for small artisan estates, chef Turi serves fresh local produce at this restaurant (see p79).

3 Chalet Clan dei Ragazzi, Linguaglossa

MAP G3 ▪ Linguaglossa ▪ 340 7350907 ▪ No credit cards ▪ €

This rustic wooden chalet, set at 1,500 m (4,900 ft) up Etna's northern slope, serves simple, authentic food. Book in advance for dinner.

4 Pepe Rosa, Bronte

MAP G3 ▪ Corso Umberto 226 ▪ 095 7724476 ▪ Closed Mon ▪ €€

Bronte is known for its pistachios, which feature in every course at this charming little family-run restaurant. Don't miss the bruschetta with pistachio pesto.

5 La Grotta, Acireale

Fresh seafood at Pepe Rosa

MAP G3 ▪ Via Scalo Grande 46 ▪ 095 7648153 ▪ Closed Tue & last two weeks in Oct ▪ €€

Set in an actual grotto, this six-table restaurant is a local favourite thanks to top-quality fish. Booking is a must.

6 Osteria Antica Marina, Catania

MAP G4 ▪ Via Pardo 29 ▪ 095 348197 ▪ Closed Wed ▪ €€€

This *osteria* in the fish market sells a selection of each day's catch. The marinated anchovies are a must-try.

PRICE CATEGORIES

For a three-course meal for one with half a bottle of wine (or equivalent meal), taxes and extra charges.

€ under €35   €€ €35–€70   €€€ over €70

Elegant dining at La Capinera

7 La Capinera, Taormina

MAP H3 ▪ Via Nazionale 177, Spisone, Taormina Mare ▪ 338 1588013 ▪ Closed Mon ▪ €€€

Pietro d'Agostino's lovely seaside restaurant is renowned for its creative fresh fish preparations, fair prices and beautiful atmosphere.

8 Trattoria da Pina, Vulcano

MAP G1 ▪ Gelso ▪ 368 668555 ▪ No credit cards ▪ Closed mid-Oct–Easter ▪ €

Good Aeolian cuisine is served on a dockside terrace at Gelso, with views to Mount Etna.

9 Ristorante Pizzeria Granduca, Taormina

MAP H3 ▪ Corso Umberto 172 ▪ 094 224983 ▪ €€

This terraced pizzeria has a lovely garden and offers sweeping views of the Mediterranean Sea.

10 Nangalarruni, Castelbuono

MAP E3 ▪ Cortile Ventimiglia 5 ▪ 092 1671228 ▪ Closed mid-Jan: Wed ▪ €€

Great mountain food, such as pork from the Nebrodi heritage breed.

See map on p108

🔟 Southwest Sicily

Beyond the beauty of the mosaics at the Villa Romana and the temples at Agrigento, sandy beaches, ruined Greek cities and olive groves feature all along the little-developed coastline of southwest Sicily. Enna dominates the wide, wheat-filled valleys, and isolated farming villages crown the hilltops, with vast expanses of rocky mountains or rolling fields in between. As a result of the lack of infrastructure and mass emigration from the region, the villages have remained almost as they were centuries ago.

Greek Temple, Agrigento

SOUTHWEST SICILY

1 Agrigento and the Valle dei Templi

The Valley of the Temples (see pp32–5) was the heart of one of the most important cities in the ancient world and is a prime example of the magnificence of Magna Graecia.

2 Sciacca
MAP C4

Dominated by Monte San Calogero and built on a terrace over the sea, this was the thermal spa town for Selinunte and still has a spa offering sulphur and mud baths.

Vase from Sciacca

The small port town has a harbour with little blue-and-white boats, a thriving ceramics tradition and a good mix of old and new. Stop to admire the Porta San Salvatore (1581), with its decorative reliefs, and the Catalan-Gothic Palazzo Steripinto, with its diamond-shaped rustication. Then walk down the Corso Vittorio Emanuele to the Piazza A Scandaliato for views down to the port, then on to the Duomo for its beautiful Baroque façade with Gagini sculptures.

3 Il Corleonese
MAP C3

The central zone around the village of Corleone is referred to as il Corleonese and has long been known for its generous water supplies and fertile soil. Remote villages are sprinkled throughout, all worth a quick visit to witness a way of life that is slow to change – visit Bisacquino, Palazzo Adriano, Cammarata, Mussomeli, Prizzi and Corleone itself, a successful modern town with a lovely historic centre.

4 Morgantina
MAP F4 ■ Open 9am–7pm daily ■ Adm

Morgantina was settled first by the Italic Morganti people, then by the Greeks in the 6th century BC, then the Romans, though it was only excavated in 1955. The large, well-preserved site comprises a split-level *agora* (forum) for town meetings, the *macellum* (covered market), large, black lava millstones, a gymnasium, a fountain with a double basin, homes with mosaic flooring, a 1,000-seat theatre and kilns for firing terracotta.

Map legend:

1 Top 10 Sights
see pp117–9

1 Places to Eat
see p123

1 Scenic Views
see p121

1 Chthonic Deities and their Sites
see p120

Madonie Mountains · Petralia Soprana · Castellana Sicula · Alimena · Resuttano · Salso · Villarosa · Santa Caterina Villarmosa · Enna **6** · A19 · Caltanissetta · **5** · Pietraperzia · Morgantina **4** · Aidone · Villa Romana del Casale **9** · San Michele di Ganzaria **3** · ommatino · Mazzarino · Gela · Riesi · Caltagirone · Butera · Maróglio · S117 · Niscemi · Falconara · Golfo di Gela · Gela

3 7 6 7 · **9 9**

0 kilometres 15
0 miles 15

Ancient settlement of Morgantina

Sandy beach at Eraclea Minoa

5 Eraclea Minoa

MAP C4 ▪ Open 8am–1 hour before sunset daily ▪ Closed 1 Jan ▪ Adm

The ruins of this ancient Greek city lie on a headland above a wide beach, above vineyards and olive groves and on the white sandstone cliffs. Midway between Selinunte and Agrigento and on the border between Carthaginian- and Greek-held territory, Eraclea Minoa saw its share of border disputes. Now, it is quiet and well kept. A small museum and groomed paths lead to an intimate theatre carved into the sandstone, remains of defensive walls with towers and the residential section where a few houses made of local stone have kept their floor and wall decorations. Since it's not on the standard tour bus route, the added pleasure of a visit is that you may have this place all to yourself.

View over Caltabellotta

6 Enna

MAP E4

Due to its easily defendable position on the top of a tall hill, Enna was almost the only town in the interior for centuries. The Greeks called it the "umbilicus of Sicily", and it was a key position for any group that wanted to take the island. Enna was so well defended that the Arabs, having tried to capture it for 20 years, resorted to crawling in through the sewer system. In the historic centre, see the Gothic Duomo with Baroque renovations and the church of San Giovanni with an Arab dome. Also visit the Museo Musical Art 3M. Once considered the geographic centre of Sicily, octagonal Frederick's Tower is 24 m (79 ft) tall and offers fine views from the top. Castello di Lombardia *(see p48)* is a mixture of Byzantine, Arab, Norman and Swabian architecture, and is among the largest and most important of Sicily's medieval castles.

7 Caltabellotta

MAP C4

This tiny village, 950 m (3,100 ft) above sea level, has a lovely medieval centre. In 1090, the already fortified village was taken from the Arabs by the Norman king Count Roger, who built the Chiesa Madre and fortified the now ruined castle. It was in this castle in 1194 that William III, the heir to the Norman throne, and his mother were held prisoner and probably murdered by Emperor Henry VI; it was also the site of the signing of the 1302 peace treaty between Frederick II of Aragón and Charles of Valois, putting an end to the Sicilian Vespers *(see p42)*.

8 Pelagie Islands
MAP B6

These are three flat islands isolated in the Mediterranean. Lampione is uninhabited, Linosa has volcanic soil and clear waters. Lampedusa has constructed modern buildings for the tourist boom but it is still good for swimming, diving and watching sea turtles, dolphins and whales (in May).

Villa Romana del Casale mosaic

9 Villa Romana del Casale
The finest surviving Roman mosaics in the world cover the floors of this official's luxurious hunting villa (see pp30–31).

10 La Scala dei Turchi
MAP D4

A popular summer destination for Sicilians, La Scala dei Turchi, near Realmonte, is a marl rock formation named for its natural harbour, which was a hideaway from the invading Turks in the 16th century. The ripples in the cliff, sculpted by the elements, are accessed via a limestone entrance. The well-worn path can be slippery.

ORANGES AND OTHER CITRUS FRUITS

Citrus fruits were introduced to Sicily by the Arabs and have been a cash crop for centuries. There are lemons, tangerines, mandarins and varieties of oranges, from sweet to sour, pale gold to dark purple. The plantations, around Ribera, are marked by their low-growing trees with dark-green leaves, bright fruits and heady fragrance.

AN AFTERNOON IN CALTABELLOTTA

Take a late afternoon drive from the bustling town of Sciacca up to sleepy **Caltabellotta**. Skip the modern outskirts of the village to wander around the narrow streets and *piazzettas* of **Terravecchia**, the old medieval centre.

Terravecchia lies on a flat plain under the **Chiesa Madre**. This Norman church was founded by Count Roger one year before he took Palermo (see pp12–13). It has been restored, so admire the entry portal with pointed arch and the bell tower which was originally an Arabic fortification. The unornamental exterior belies the inside of this church where you can see the *Madonna of the Chain, St Benedict* and *Madonna and Child* – all works by the artist Gagini.

On the other side of the plain, opposite the Chiesa Madre, find the church of **San Salvatore** (see p117) with its zigzag decoration around the door.

To the north of the church, use the steps carved out of the rock to climb up to the highest point of Monte Castello. Walk around the ruins of Count Roger's castle, with its single Gothic doorway, and take in one of the most stunning views in Sicily. You can see the coastline to the south from **Agrigento** (see pp32–5) to **Marsala** (see p101).

Back in Caltabellotta, stroll from Piazza Umberto I to Via Roma in the newer part of the village, where you can have an excellent dinner of traditional Sicilian mountain fare at the cosy **La Ferla** (see p123) trattoria.

See map on pp116–17

Chthonic Deities and their Sites

1 Demeter
The cult of the Mother Goddess, the protector of agriculture and fertility, is one of the most ancient in Sicily. When her daughter Persephone went missing, Demeter roamed the Earth searching for her, ignoring the crops and causing a famine.

Bust of Demeter dated 500–450 BC

2 Persephone
The daughter of Demeter and Zeus (also known as Kore or, to the Romans, Proserpine) rules as both queen of the underworld and goddess of fertility.

3 Persephone's Abduction
While gathering flowers with her girlfriends in fields below Enna, Persephone was abducted by Hades to reign as queen of the underworld.

Persephone returns to Earth

4 Persephone's Return
Hades freed Persephone but she had to eat a pomegranate seed, which would ensure her return to the underworld for four months a year. For four months it is winter on Earth; when she returns, it is spring.

5 Lago di Pergusa
A deep natural lake south of Enna is the supposed site of the passage from Earth to the underworld.

6 Sanctuary at Enna
The seat of the cult of Demeter and Persephone was based at Enna on the boulder behind the castle. Their temple contained a statue of the Mother Goddess (Demeter).

7 Votive Offerings from the Sanctuary at Enna
MAP E4 ■ Museo Archeologico, Palazzo Varisano, Piazza Mazzini ■ Open 9am–7pm daily ■ Adm
Items recovered from the sanctuary and from sites near Lake Pergusa are preserved in Enna's Museo Archeologico, including votive statuettes of Demeter.

8 Rock Sanctuary of Demeter, Agrigento
The Earth goddesses were venerated at a walled sanctuary in Agrigento, which is now marked by the church of San Biagio. The church was built on top of a 5th-century BC temple, of which two round altars remain.

9 Sanctuary at Morgantina
Demeter and Persephone were worshipped as the protectors of Morgantina. In the sanctuary it is possible to see purification baths, altars for performing rituals and a well for sacred offerings.

10 Sanctuary at Palma di Montechiaro
Three small 7th-century-BC votive statuettes of the goddesses Demeter or Persephone are now in the archaeological museum in Syracuse. They were recovered from the sanctuary of Palma di Montechiaro, between Agrigento and Gela.

See map on pp116–17

Scenic Views

1 From Caltabellotta
MAP C4

From the ruins of the Norman castle above Caltabellotta *(see pp118–19)* you can see all the way to the flat coast towards Marsala and the hilly interior dotted with villages and farms.

2 Prizzi
MAP D3

Driving through the Corleonese zone *(see p117)*, Prizzi is one of the highest towns, covering the top of its hill like a *coppola* (peasant farmer's cap).

3 Views from Enna
MAP E4

From the Piazza Crispi, see across the deep valley to Calascibetta on the flat top of its own terraced hill, as well as across the interior all the way to Mount Etna.

4 Sutera

Set amid the Sikanian hills, Sutera affords sweeping vistas to the Mediterranean and Mount Etna, with fields of wheat below. Spring is pretty when there are wildflowers such as sulla, poppies and buttercups.

5 The Valle dei Templi by Night

Agrigento's temples are romantic at night. Attractive from any vantage point, perhaps the finest view is from the terrace of the restaurant Accademia del Buon Gusto, with the Temple of Concord *(see pp32–5)* as a backdrop.

6 Countryside around Il Corleonese

Vast expanses of rolling terrain around Il Corleonese *(see p117)* are planted with wheat, vines, olives and artichokes. There are blankets of crimson sulla, red poppies and yellow fennel growing impossibly tall.

7 Vallate near Enna
MAP E4

The enormous fertile *vallate* (valleys) around Enna are planted with wheat, and the spectacular stretches of soft golden fields change colour with the seasons, from lush green, to pale yellow, to black.

8 The Rocca di Nadore
MAP C4

The round-topped Rocca di Nadore above Sciacca turns its flat, white face towards the sea and dominates the coast for miles. See it looming on the horizon as far away as Selinunte.

9 From Morgantina

From the residential sector of the ancient site *(see p117)* on the east hill, look down on the *agora* (forum) and out towards the east coast and the outline of Mount Etna.

10 From Eraclea Minoa

From the ruins of Eraclea Minoa *(see p118)* on top of a striking white sandstone cliff, look down towards the wide stretch of sandy beach and the dark sea below.

The Temple of Concord

Local Produce

Vineyards, Regaleali

1 Wine
During the 20th century large estates growing wheat and other crops also started to cultivate vines to produce high-quality wine. Two good examples are Regaleali *(see p75)* near Vallelunga and Planeta near Sambuca di Sicilia.

2 Oranges
Ribera is well known for its production of the prized Washington variety of navel orange, introduced to the area by emigrants returning from North America.

3 Co-operative Produce
In and around Corleone *(see p117)*, several co-operatives under the umbrella *Libera Terra* cultivate land confiscated from Mafia bosses to create jobs and strengthen the economy of the area. Wheat is grown for pasta, grapes for wine, along with fruits, cheeses and honey.

4 Preserved Fish
Preserved tuna was a staple food for centuries on ships sailing the Mediterranean, and tuna are still big business. At Sciacca, anchovies and sardines are processed by hand and packed under salt or olive oil for export all over the world.

5 Olive Oil
Cities such as Castelvetrano and Trapani are famous for their olives. The harvest begins in October, and first pressings of the extra virgin olive oil are available from the end of November. Towns celebrate the new season's oil with tastings.

6 Fresh Fish
Fishing villages line Sicily's southern coast, with centres at Licata, Porto Empedocle and Sciacca.

7 Wheat
Latifondi (large estates owned by nobility) took up much of the interior until well into the 20th century. Today, vast valleys and hills are devoted to cultivating Sicily's special wheat, *grano duro (see p77)*, which is an important source of income.

8 Cheese
Sicily is renowned for its cheeses, made from both cow and sheep's milk. Look for the sharp Caciocavallo Ragusano, the saffron-infused Piacentino di Enna and the soft Vastedda del Belice.

9 Broad Beans
Large broad beans, or *fave*, are cultivated in the countryside near Enna. They are eaten dressed with olive oil or used in soups.

10 Artichokes
A staple of Sicilian cuisine, they are at their best in spring. Cerda has a three-day artichoke festival in April.

Artichokes for sale

Places to Eat

① La Madia, Licata
MAP E5 ▪ Corso F Re Capriata 22 ▪ 092 2771443 ▪ Closed Tue, Sun dinner, Jun–mid-Sep: Sun lunch ▪ €€€

Chef Pino Cuttaia is dedicated to seasonality at this two Michelin-starred restaurant *(see p79)* in Licata.

② Trattoria dei Templi, Agrigento
MAP D4 ▪ Via Panoramica dei Templi 15 ▪ 092 2403110 ▪ €

This family-run trattoria has an excellent Sicilian menu: try pasta with swordfish and mint.

Pasta alla Norma

③ Ristorante Pomara, San Michele di Ganzaria
MAP F4 ▪ Via Vittorio Veneto 84 ▪ 093 3978143 ▪ €

The stone fireplace in this restaurant is where local cheeses, vegetables as well as meats are grilled for hearty dishes such as pasta with pistachios.

④ Ristorante Gennaro, Corleone
MAP C3 ▪ Corso Dei Mille 132 ▪ 091 8464767 ▪ Closed Mon ▪ €€

Run by a couple, this restaurant serves traditional Sicilian cuisine and pizzas, alongside artisanal craft beer.

⑤ Osteria il Grappolo, Sciacca
MAP C4 ▪ Via Conzo 9/A ▪ 092 585294 ▪ Closed Mon ▪ €

Sicilian dishes here are made with products from the family's small farm and the fish is fresh from the sea.

⑥ Porto San Paolo, Sciacca
MAP C4 ▪ Largo San Paolo 1 ▪ 092 527982 ▪ Closed Wed & 24 Dec ▪ €€

The daily catch is cooked in typical Mediterranean style. Terrace tables look over Sciacca's small port.

PRICE CATEGORIES
For a three-course meal for one with half a bottle of wine (or equivalent meal), taxes and extra charges.
....
€ under €35   €€ €35–€70   €€€ over €70

---

⑦ La Lanterna, Milena
MAP D4 ▪ Corso Pietro Nenni 8 ▪ 093 4933478 ▪ Closed Mon ▪ €

This trattoria serves traditional Sicilian food. Try their set menu.

⑧ La Ferla, Caltabellotta
MAP C4 ▪ Via Roma 29 ▪ 092 5951444 ▪ Closed Mon, Oct ▪ €

With stunning sea views, this place is a local favourite. Try the roasted artichokes and local cheeses.

⑨ Capitolo Primo del Relais Briuccia, Agrigento
MAP D4 ▪ Via Trieste 1, Montallegro ▪ 092 2847755 ▪ Closed Mon ▪ €€

Creative versions of Sicilian dishes with items from wild fennel to saffron.

Capitolo Primo del Relais Briuccia

⑩ Ruga Reali, Agrigento
MAP D4 ▪ Cortile Scribani 8 ▪ 092 220370 ▪ €

An informal *osteria* popular with locals and specializing in fish dishes. The 15th-century building has beams and a courtyard for alfresco dining.

See map on pp116–17

🔟 Southeast Sicily

Baroque ornamentation

The landscape of the southeast is different from the rest of the island. Here, the white limestone strata with scrubland is broken by steep gorges and low dry-stone walls. The Greek and Roman remains at Syracuse are spectacular, while Caltagirone, Modica, Noto, Palazzolo Acreide, Ragusa and Scicli have all been declared World Heritage Sites thanks to their Baroque architecture and urban planning. There is also a gastronomic renaissance taking place in this area. Seafood from the coastal zones, along with meat, cheese and wild greens from the interior are being used by young chefs aware that old traditions and even ingredients are on the brink of extinction. They are returning to their roots and preserving and revitalizing the authentic cuisine of the region.

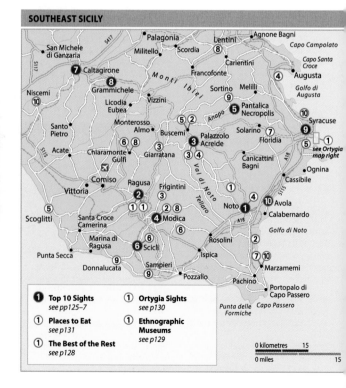

SOUTHEAST SICILY

Legend:
- **1** Top 10 Sights *see pp125–7*
- **1** Places to Eat *see p131*
- **1** The Best of the Rest *see p128*
- **1** Ortygia Sights *see p130*
- **1** Ethnographic Museums *see p129*

0 kilometres 15
0 miles 15

Spectacular location of Ragusa Ibla

1 Noto

Noto *(see pp28–9)* was rebuilt in Baroque style after the earthquake of 1693, using a tufa stone that has turned a golden shade. There are wide streets and plenty of piazzas and *piazzettas* for the *passeggiata*.

Ortygia, Syracuse

0 metres 250
0 yards 250

2 Ragusa
MAP F5

Ragusa was founded as Hybla Heraia by the Sicels. After the earthquake of 1693, half the population rebuilt on the ridge above (Ragusa) while the other half renovated the old village (Ragusa Ibla). Ibla has a dramatic location with its buildings clinging to the side of a cliff. The Duomo, stands at the top of a stairway in the heart of town, while the oval-shaped church of San Giuseppe has another striking Baroque façade.

Greek Theatre, Palazzolo Acreide

3 Palazzolo Acreide
MAP G5

This Baroque town *(see p58)* was originally a Greek colony of Syracuse, founded in 664 BC. Next to the town, the 600-seat Greek theatre remains in good condition, although the temples to Persephone and Aphrodite are in ruins. A short walk from the old city is I Santoni, a sanctuary dedicated to the fertility goddess Cybele.

4 Modica
MAP G6

Rebuilt after 1693, on and between two deep gorges, the city is divided in two parts – Modica Alta, the upper town, and Modica Bassa, the lower town. Founded by the Sicels, the city fell under Spanish rule, when it was the capital of a quasi-autonomous state ruled by Spanish barons. The lively Corso Umberto I, with cafés, boutiques, pastry shops, numerous palaces and a theatre, crosses Modica Bassa. Also on this street is a monumental flight of steps with fine Baroque statues of the Apostles that leads up to the post-1693 church dedicated to San Pietro. Up the hill, Modica Alta's Baroque Duomo di San Giorgio is attributed to Gagliardi.

Pantalica Necropolis

5 Pantalica Necropolis
MAP G5

Pantalica was at the heart of ancient Hybla (known through its striking red-glazed pottery, examples of which are on view in Syracuse). The Anapo River carved a gorge through the limestone, creating what became Sicily's largest necropolis; there are more than 8,000 tombs here. A hike through the gorge takes you past thousands of burial sites, carved into the cliff sides, as well as wild orchids, rabbits, porcupines, falcons and the remains of a medieval settlement.

6 Scicli
MAP F6

Dominated by a high, rocky cliff, Scicli was an outpost of the Spanish barons during their long reign over the County of Modica. From the wide

CAROB TREES

Huge *carrubi* (carob trees) are a feature of southeast Sicily. The trees produce a fruit shaped like a brown pea pod, with sweet flesh and small, hard seeds. The seeds are amazingly uniform and were the original carat used to weigh precious stones. Carob's sweet flesh can be used in pasta and sweets. Once called "poor man's chocolate", the deep, rich flavour is now prized by chefs.

Piazza Italia, the Via Nazionale passes the street where the Palazzo Beneventano sits on a corner, its sculpture now weathered by the elements. Via Nazionale continues to Piazza Busacca, with views into the older, residential section of town, with its narrow lanes and terracotta roofs.

7 Caltagirone
MAP F4

Named after the Arabic *Cal'at Ghiran* (Castle of Vases), ceramic production has been the main industry in this town since prehistoric times (visit the local Museo della Ceramica). The Baroque town built onto the hillside is a pleasure to wander through, with alleyways, cafés and ceramics shops. A stairway leads from the lower town up to the church of Santa Maria del Monte, and each of the 142 steps is decorated with majolica tiles.

Tiled steps to Santa Maria del Monte

8 Grammichele
MAP F5

Built by the Principe di Butera after the 1693 earthquake to house the farmers of the destroyed town of Occhiolà, there is an authentic peasant-farmer feel here, though it was built on a grand plan inspired by Renaissance mathematical ideals. Concentric hexagonals radiate from around the central Piazza Umberto I, home to private residences, *palazzi*, the Chiesa Madre and the town hall.

Façade of the cathedral, Syracuse

9 Syracuse

The remains of the mighty powerhouse of Magna Graecia make up some of the most important sites in Sicily, while the small historic centre of Ortygia (see p130) is one of the most pleasant town centres on this island (see pp24–7).

10 Avola
MAP G5

The almond-growing capital of Italy, Avola also lends its name to one of the best-known red wines produced in Sicily. Dating back to the prehistoric Sicanian era, Avola was a predominantly Greco-Roman city and artifacts from these eras can be seen in the small Roman villa and megalithic dolmen. Facing the Ionian Sea, it is a charming town with quaint Baroque buildings and sandy beaches. Visit the Cava di Cassibile nature reserve, home to a rare species of orchid.

A DAY IN MODICA AND RAGUSA IBLA

▶ MORNING

Spend a morning in **Modica**, stopping by the **Cathedral of San Giorgio of Modica Alta** (see p47) on your way into town. In Modica Bassa, visit the equally splendid Sicilian Baroque church of **San Pietro**. Walk down the Corso Umberto I towards Duomo di San Giorgio, passing cafés, shops and buildings that incorporate parts of pre-earthquake structures. Stop by **Antica Dolceria Bonajuto** (Corso Umberto I 159), the oldest chocolate factory in Sicily, to taste and buy a wide range of Modica's traditional sweets including, 'Mpanatigghi (see p81).

Drive along the SS 115 to Ragusa (see p125). On the way, you will cross a viaduct, which is one of the tallest of its kind in Europe, before travelling into a fertile land of citrus groves and carob trees. In Giardini Iblei park, pick up a map of the maze-like streets from the information office. Next door, have lunch at **Ristorante Duomo** (see p131).

AFTERNOON

Spend the afternoon wandering through **Ragusa Ibla** (see p125) to see the **Duomo di San Giorgio** and the church of San Giuseppe. You can study the Baroque façade of the Duomo from the lively piazza with a treat from **Gelati DiVini** (Piazza Duomo 20) – their ice cream is made from Sicilian wines. But don't fail to walk through the narrow side streets, where tiny alleys are connected with staircases and tunnels, for a taste of authentic Ragusa Ibla.

See map on pp124–5

The Best of the Rest

① Noto Antica
MAP G5

To the northwest of Noto lie the evocative ruins of the old pre-earthquake town. Built on an arid, limestone ridge, the site commands views of the Ragusan plain and Mount Etna. Under the hot Sicilian sun, purple thistle and sun-dried herbs perfume the air.

Cave rooms in Noto Antica

② Vendicari
MAP G6

The reserve's maquis supports thyme, rosemary and juniper; the wetlands host migratory birds. Depending on the season, watch for herons, egrets and flamingoes.

③ Giarratana
MAP G5

The narrow streets of this tiny town in the middle of the Monte Iblei are lined with residences, palaces and churches. The typical low doors protect against cold winter winds.

④ Megara Iblea
MAP G5

Lovely and extensive coastal remains of a town founded in 728 BC by Greek colonists from Megara, near Athens.

⑤ Ciane River
MAP G5

The river's source is said to be a pool formed by the tears of Cyane, who tried to prevent Persephone's abduction into the underworld. The river banks are thick with papyrus. Take a boat tour past the Olympieion.

⑥ Cave d'Ispica
MAP G6

An ancient river carved out this gorge, now an open-air park with excellent walks and climbs. The cliff sides are hollowed out to form ancient tombs of religious hermits; in one cave is a Byzantine fresco of the Madonna.

⑦ Marzamemi
MAP G6

This little fishing village grew up around the *tonnara* (tuna fishery) and villa of the noble Villadorata family. Modern resort features, including popular nightclubs, have been added.

⑧ Lentini
MAP G4

The excavations of this small, but important and powerful former Greek colony are worth exploring.

⑨ Sampieri
MAP F6

Clear waters and sandy beaches surround what was once a small fishing village. The beaches at Punta Pisciotto are accessed from a turn-off at the abandoned, temple-like brick kilns called Fornace Penna.

⑩ Castello Eurialo
MAP G5

This Greek military castle (see p49) was built in 402 BC and is notable for its 15-m (50-ft) keep. Walk the path on the northern side for views of the fortress and coast (see p25).

Castello Eurialo fortifications

Ethnographic Museums

1 **Museo del Tempo Contadino, Ragusa**

MAP F5 ■ Palazzo Zacco, Via San Vito 158 ■ Open Sat & Sun ■ Adm

Palazzo Zacco houses a collection of historic farming and farm kitchen tools, lace and embroidery work.

2 **I Luoghi del Lavoro Contadino, Buscemi**

MAP G5 ■ Via Libertà 10 ■ Open 8am–1pm Mon–Fri (to noon Sat) ■ Adm

Buscemi is a living museum. Eight workrooms and living spaces, including the home of a peasant farmer, a smithy and a mill, have been faithfully preserved.

I Luoghi del Lavoro Contadino

3 **Casa-Museo di Antonino Uccello, Palazzolo Acreide**

MAP G5 ■ Via Machiavelli 19 ■ Open 9am–7pm Mon–Sat, 2–7pm Sun ■ Adm

This museum *(see p51)* displays handmade objects created by Sicilian peasant farmers.

4 **Mulino ad Acqua Santa Lucia, Palazzolo Acreide**

MAP G5 ■ Valle dei Mulini 10 ■ 338 2415910 ■ Open by appt only ■ Adm

Antique water-powered grain mill complete with working millstones.

5 **Centro di Documentazione della Vita Popolare Iblea, Buscemi**

MAP G5 ■ Via Vittorio Emanuele ■ Open 8:30am–1:30pm Mon–Sat ■ Adm

The centre preserves 180 hours of film and 12,000 prints, which document agricultural life.

6 **Museo del Costume, Scicli**

MAP F6 ■ Via Francesco Mormina Penna 65 ■ Open 10:30am–12:30pm & 4:30–8pm Tue–Sat

The museum is dedicated to keeping alive the history and culture of the Iblean mountain communities.

7 **Museo della Civiltà Contadina Iblea, Floridia**

MAP G5 ■ Piazza Umberto I 27 ■ Open 5–8pm Mon–Fri, by appt Sun ■ Adm

Mills for wheat and olives, looms and a range of tools have been collected from farmers' homes throughout the Iblean countryside.

8 **Museo del Ricamo e dello Sfilato, Chiaramonte Gulfi**

MAP F5 ■ Via Laurea 4 ■ Open 8:30am–1:30pm Mon–Fri, 10am–1pm Sat, Sun & hols ■ Adm

Antique looms and instruments for producing thread and cloth are here.

9 **A Casa do Fascitraru, Sortino**

MAP G5 ■ Via Gioberti 5 ■ Open by appt ■ 093 1952992 ■ Adm

Sortino is well known for its bee-keeping tradition. This museum displays beekeeping and honey-making implements.

10 **Museo di Civiltà Contadina Angelo Marsiano, Niscemi**

MAP F5 ■ Via Mazzini 78 ■ Opening hours vary, call ahead ■ 093 3881111

Displays on life in the Sicilian countryside and traditional crafts.

See map on pp124–5

Ortygia Sights

1 Ortygia
MAP H5

The tiny island is a bustling mix of temples, churches, museums, open piazzas, seaside bars, markets and shops. It is also lively after hours.

2 Temple of Apollo
On Largo XXV Luglio are the remains of the Doric Temple of Apollo (see p25). Built in 575 BC, this was the first temple in Sicily with an exterior stone colonnade. Two monolithic sandstone columns remain.

3 Duomo
One of the most spectacular buildings in Sicily, the dramatic Baroque façade fronts a 5th-century-BC Doric temple. It was transformed into a church in the 7th century AD. Clearly visible inside and out are monolithic Doric columns.

4 Piazzetta San Rocco
This piazza and the network of streets around it are the hub of Ortygia's nightlife.

5 Via Maestranza
Now lined with boutiques and restaurants, this street was where noble families built their Baroque palaces, which often incorporated older structures.

6 Piazza del Duomo
Excavations in this square have unearthed the remains of 8th-century BC houses from the original Sicel culture. Around the piazza are the Duomo, the town hall (located atop an Ionic Temple to Artemis) and cafés.

7 The Greek Ghetto
The six streets between Via della Giudecca and Via GB Alagona follow the Greek urban plan. The area is still crowded with medieval houses and laundry drying in the breeze.

8 Fonte Aretusa
The mythical Arethusa (see p43) was turned into a spring and bubbles up on the shores of lower Ortygia. Along the Lungomare Alfeo, a terrace looks down on the spring that now feeds into a pond, with ducks and tall papyrus.

9 Castello Maniace
093 14508211 ▪ Open 8:30am–7:30pm daily (by appt only) ▪ Adm

Frederick II built this castle around 1239. Castello Maniace takes its name from the Byzantine George Maniakes who "liberated" Syracuse during the 11th century.

10 Market
Via del Mercato & Via Trento ▪ Open Mon–Sat am

The market bustles with local shoppers and vendors yelling out the merits of their wares. Farmers and fishermen heap tomatoes, mussels, cherries and more into colourful mounds to entice local customers.

Piazza del Duomo, Ortygia

Places to Eat

PRICE CATEGORIES

For a three-course meal for one with half a bottle of wine (or equivalent meal), taxes and extra charges.

€ under €35   €€ €35–€70   €€€ over €70

1 Ristorante Duomo, Ragusa Ibla

MAP F5 ▪ Via Capitano Bocchieri 31 ▪ 093 2651265 ▪ Closed Jan–Feb, Mon lunch & Sun ▪ €€€

Ciccio Sultano expertly chooses local ingredients (see p79). The traditional Ragusan food is served in an elegant dining room.

2 Singola, Modica

MAP G6 ▪ Via Risorgimento 88 ▪ 093 2904807 ▪ Closed Mon lunch & Tue ▪ €€

Singola uses fresh ingredients in season from local farms, which are organic when possible, in its creative vegetarian and vegan dishes. There's also a great atmosphere here.

3 Ristorante Fidone Maria, Frigintini

MAP G5 ▪ Via Gianforma 6 ▪ 093 2901135 ▪ Closed Mon ▪ €

At this much-loved family-run trattoria (see p78) near Ragusa, everything is prepared in house, and it's all excellent.

4 Ristorante Crocifisso, Noto

MAP G5 ▪ Via Principe Umberto 48 ▪ 093 1968608 ▪ Closed Jan & Feb ▪ €€

This family-run restaurant offers recipes such as *coniglio stimperata* (sweet-and-sour rabbit), fried ricotta, and ravioli in pork *ragù*.

5 Sakalleo, Scoglitti

MAP F5 ▪ Piazza Cavour 12 ▪ 093 2871688 ▪ €€

The menu depends upon what the fishing boats bring in. The animated owner may also have a glass of wine with you.

6 Majore, Chiaramonte Gulfi

MAP F5 ▪ Via Martiri Ungheresi 12 ▪ 093 2928019 ▪ Closed Mon ▪ €

Enjoy a variety of typical Hyblaean dishes at this highly popular restaurant (see p78).

Fresh fish at La Darsena da Ianuzzo

7 La Darsena da Ianuzzo, Syracuse

MAP H5 ▪ Riva Garibaldi 6, Ortygia ▪ 093 166104 ▪ Closed Mon ▪ €€

Feast on fresh fish, perfectly and traditionally cooked, in the dining room or the waterfront terrace.

8 Accursio, Modica

MAP G6 ▪ Via Grimaldi 41 ▪ 093 2941689 ▪ Closed Sun dinner & Mon ▪ €€€

Michelin-starred restaurant (see p79) offering creative Sicilian cuisine.

9 Mezzaparola, Donnalucata

MAP F6 ▪ Via Martiri d'Ungheria, 2 ▪ 093 2937474 ▪ €€

This waterfront spot specializes in freshly dipped and fried sardines – a local delicacy.

10 La Cialoma, Marzamemi

MAP G6 ▪ Piazza Regina Margherita 23 ▪ 093 1841772 ▪ Closed Dec–May: Tue, Nov ▪ €€€

Enthusiastic service, a tasty, mainly fish-based menu and a great wine list are served in this romantic square (see p78) with live music in summer.

See map on pp124–5

Streetsmart

Colourful traditional Sicilian
painted plates

Getting Around

Arriving by Air

Sicily's four international airports are situated in Catania, Palermo, Trapani and Comiso and have excellent links to the nearest city centre as well as to smaller villages. **Aeroporto di Catania-Fontanarossa** is 6 km (4 miles) from the city centre, best reached by the **Alibus** shuttle. Tickets can be bought on board. Major coach companies, including **Ast**, **Sais** and **Etnabus**, stop outside the arrivals hall and provide excellent links to out-of-town destinations. Taxis into town start at €25.

Palermo's **Aeroporto Falcone-Borsellino** is roughly 35 km (22 miles) from the city centre. The **Prestia e Comandè** bus service will take you to the centre in 40 minutes; tickets can be purchased online or on board. Taxis to the centre start at €45. Two trains run between the airport and Palermo's Stazione Centrale every hour and the journey takes 60 minutes.

The west coast of Sicily is served by **Aeroporto di Trapani-Birgi**. A regular shuttle service into the city centre is run by Ast, while taxis start at €30.

The southeast is served by the **Aeroporto Pio La Torre** in Comiso. Bus company **Tumino** has a service to Ragusa, with stops in towns along the way. Ast and Etnabus run a good service to other destinations in the southeast. Taxis to Ragusa start at €32. Sicily also has the **Aeroporto di**

Pantelleria and the **Aeroporto di Lampedusa** serving domestic traffic.

International Train Travel

If you are planning on reaching Sicily by train from abroad, you will first have to cross the whole Italian peninsula which will take at least 14 hours. When buying your ticket, make sure you reserve a seat (or a sleeping compartment), as trains can get very crowded in high season.

Once in Villa San Giovanni, the train is boarded onto a ferry and passengers are asked to get off, even in the night. Make sure to take your valuables with you.

You can buy tickets and passes for multiple journeys around Italy and Europe via **Eurail** or **Interrail**. However, you may still need to pay an additional reservation fee depending on which rail service you travel with. Check that your pass is valid before boarding.

Domestic Train Travel

Given the varied and often mountainous topography of Sicily, remote areas are not accessible by train, and the very few train lines in those areas can be slow and unreliable. They are, however, more comfortable than coaches, and in addition offer views of some of the prettiest landscapes in Sicily. All the main train lines in Sicily are run by

Trenitalia, Italy's main railway operator. Tickets can be bought online and must be validated before boarding by stamping them in machines at the entrance to platforms, unless you have an e-ticket with a PNR code. Heavy fines are levied if you are caught with an unvalidated ticket.

The island's two main railway routes run between Messina and Syracuse via Catania, and from Messina to Palermo along the northern coast. A second line branches from the Messina–Palermo route at Termini Imerese, running southwards to Agrigento. Another line connects Palermo with Trapani. North of Catania, the privately operated **Ferrovia Circumetnea** line runs around Mount Etna, offering travellers a scenic route.

If you are travelling on the Messina-Palermo or Syracuse-Messina lines remember to make sure that the ticket does not require you to get a *supplemento rapido* – a surcharge that is applied to some express trains. The validity of tickets is usually two to six hours depending on the length of the journey.

Public Transport

Bus services in Sicilian cities are reliable and user-friendly. In Palermo the transport network is operated by **AMAT**, in Catania by the **AMT** and in Messina by the **ATM**. The operator websites give safety and hygiene measures, timetables, ticket information and transport maps.

Tickets can be bought at tobacconists *(tabaccai)*, news stands *(edicola)* or from special transport kiosks that also provide transport maps. Tickets are timed and are valid 90 or 120 minutes, and need to be validated in the yellow machines on the bus. Day tickets are usually very cheap and are often the best option for visitors.

Long-Distance Bus Travel

The three lines – **SAIS**, **AST** and **Etna Trasporti** – cover the entire island, while services such as **Flixbus** and **Eurolines** connect the island to the rest of Italy. There are stops to all major Sicilian cities and towns, but services are not usually direct, so you will need to change buses once or twice along the way. Travelling by coach seems to be the preference for many Sicilians, especially commuters and students, as it connects big cities with remote towns and villages that are not served by rail. Fares are very reasonable. You can usually buy tickets on board for long-haul buses *(pullman* or *corriera)* between towns and cities.

Services often depart from outside main railway stations or from a town's main piazza. In rural areas, always check bus stops for timetables and the details of local transport companies.

Taxis

Taxis are not hailed; take one at an official taxi stand (usually found at the station or close to tourist sights), or reserve one by phone. When you order a taxi by phone, the meter will run from your call.

Only accept rides in licensed, metered taxis. Official taxis are white, have a "taxi" sign on the roof and their offcial taxi licence number on the doors. Extra charges are added for each piece of luggage placed in the boot, for rides between approximately 10pm and 7am, on Sundays and public holidays, and for journeys to and from the airports. **Radiotaxi Catania**, **Radiotaxi Messina** and **Radiotaxi Palermo** are reliable.

DIRECTORY

ARRIVING BY AIR

Aeroporto di Catania-Fontanarossa
W aeroporto.catania.it

Aeroporto di Lampedusa
W aeroportodi lampedusa.com

Aeroporto di Pantelleria
W aeroportodi pantelleria.it

Aeroporto di Trapani-Birgi
W airgest.it

Aeroporto Falcone-Borsellino
W gesap.it

Aeroporto Pio La Torre (Comiso)
W aeroportodi comiso.eu

Alibus
W sitabus.it

Ast
W aziendasiciliana trasporti.it

Etnabus
W etnatrasporti.it

Prestia e Comandè
W prestiaecomande.it

Sais
W saisautolinee.it

Tumino
W tuminobus.it

INTERNATIONAL TRAIN TRAVEL

Eurail
W eurail.com

Interrail
W interrail.eu

DOMESTIC TRAIN TRAVEL

Ferrovia Circumetnea
W circumetnea.it

Trenitalia
W trenitalia.com

PUBLIC TRANSPORT

AMAT (Palermo)
W amat.pa.it

AMT (Catania)
W amt.ct.it

ATM (Messina)
W atmmessinaspa.it

LONG-DISTANCE BUS TRAVEL

AST
W aziendasiciliana trasporti.it

Etna Trasporti
W etnatrasporti.it

Eurolines
W at.eurolines.com

Flixbus
W flixbus.it

SAIS
W saisautolinee.it

TAXIS

Radiotaxi Catania
(095 8833

Radiotaxi Messina
(090 6505

Radiotaxi Palermo
(091 8481

Driving

For those eager to discover Sicily's lesser-known parts or its rural areas, travelling by car is the best option. Make sure you have all the necessary documents with you, as traffic police (carabinieri) carry out routine checks.

The drive to Sicily from Rome takes around eight hours and around six hours from Naples. Car ferries going across the Strait of Messina leave regularly. Allow one hour for the ferry ride, including waiting times and boarding.

If you bring your own foreign-registered car into the country, you must carry a Green Card, the vehicle's registration documents and have a valid driver's licence with you when driving. Many towns and cities enforce a Limited Traffic Zone (**ZTL**). To avoid fines, consult one of the **Urban Access Regulations in Europe** websites.

Sicily has a good system of highways that reaches all the major cities; most highways are toll free. Tolls are payable on most motorways (autostrade), and payment is made at the end of the journey. Avoid tolls by using the national roads (strade nazionali), or secondary state roads (strade statali). Although less direct, they are often more scenic, allowing you to stop at viewpoints and places of interest en route.

Roads known as white roads (strade bianche) have only a gravel surface. These are often narrow and steep, but are usually passable to cars. Always check your route before travelling.

To help plan your drives, the **ViaMichelin** website has maps and routes.

Car Rental

To rent a car in Sicily you must be at least 21 years old (some renters insist on a minimum age of 25) and have held a valid licence for at least a year.

Driving licences issued by any EU member states are valid throughout Italy. If visiting from outside the EU, you may need to apply for an International Driving Permit (IDP). Check with your local automobile association. Major international car rental agencies have outlets at Sicily's main airports and major towns.

Rules of the Road

Drive on the right, use the left lane only for passing, and yield to traffic from the right. Seat belts are required for all passengers, and heavy fines are levied for using a mobile phone while driving. A strict drink-drive limit (see p139) is enforced.

During the day dipped headlights are compulsory when driving on motorways, dual carriageways and on all out-of-town roads. A red warning triangle, spare tyre and fluorescent vests must be carried at all times, for use in case of an emergency. In the event of an accident or breakdown switch on your hazard warning lights and place your warning triangle 50 m (55 yd) behind your vehicle.

For breakdowns call the **ACI** emergency number (116) or the emergency services. The ACI will tow any foreign-registered vehicle to the nearest ACI-affiliated garage, free of charge if you are a member of a similar, affiliated club.

In the major cities such as Palermo or Catania it is advisable to park your car in a guarded parking area with a custodian, especially if you have your belongings in the car. If you are parking your car on the street make sure that there are no parking meters for that zone, otherwise you will have to pay a parking fine.

Hitchhiking

Hitchhiking, or autostop, is illegal on motorways, but in more rural areas it is a common way for tourists and backpackers to get around on a budget. Always consider your own safety before entering an unknown vehicle.

Scooter

A scooter offers more freedom than a car, but it can take strong nerves to drive one in cities like Palermo or Catania, with their hair-raising traffic. If you're up to it, **Rental Motor Bike** offers good deals in major cities.

Cycling

Sicily's internal roads are fairly quiet and suitable for cycling. There are many scenic routes along the coast and around Mount Etna. However, Sicilian drivers are not used to seeing cyclists on the road, so stay alert at all times. Helmets and high-visibility clothing are not obligatory but wearing them is strongly advised. You can find traffic-free city centres in towns like Syracuse and Ragusa. **Sicily Cycling** maps the best cycling routes.

Social Bike Palermo offers touring and city bikes for rent in Palermo, while **Etna Sicily Touring** rents bicycles in Catania.

Several companies operate guided and self-guided bike tours. Those such as **Ciclofree**, **Sicily Biking Tours** or **Ciclabili Siciliane** offer different types of adventures and excursions, providing you with bicycles and with the added convenience of vans carrying your luggage.

Boats and Ferries

Reggio Calabria is the principal mainland port for ferry services to Sicily with **Caronte & Tourist**. **Tirrenia** offers ferries between Palermo, Genoa and Naples. In summer, car ferries operate between Messina and Naples. Ferry services between the Sicilian islands are well organized and run regularly. Services are offered by several companies, such as **Liberty Lines** and **SNAV** *(Società Navigazione Alta Velocità)*. Ferries *(traghetti)* and hydrofoils *(aliscafi)* can get quite crowded in summer and might skip some crossings if the weather is bad.

Sailing around the Aeolian and Aegadian islands and visiting Sicily's ports is a great way to see some of the island's most breathtaking scenery.

If you are looking for the ultimate sea vacation, **Sailing Sicily** rents out catamarans and sailboats, complete with a crew of sailors. **Pasqualo** is a great option for small boats to circumnavigate the active volcano of Stromboli. You may even see it erupt.

Walking

The best way to take in a city is usually on foot because it will provide an opportunity to discover a wealth of unexpected or hidden-away sights. The city centres in many of Sicily's towns are usually compact, with key sites within easy reach of each other. Syracuse, Catania, Palermo and many more Sicilian towns have large pedestrian areas and are best enjoyed on foot. However, bear in mind that there can be a lot of ground to cover. Palermo's historical city centre covers 2.5 sq km (1 sq mile), and many of the archaeological sights involve uphill climbs. Pace yourself accordingly, and wear footwear that is both sturdy and comfortable.

Sicily also offers many opportunities for scenic hikes, both in the countryside, on Mount Etna or in nature reserves, and expert guides are often available to help you plan your route or take you. **Outdoor Active** is a great source for finding your perfect hiking trail. **Sicilia Outdoor** is another useful website for planning walks and hikes. Always make sure you bring enough water, and wear sturdy shoes and a hat, as the sun can be very strong.

DIRECTORY

DRIVING

ViaMichelin
w viamichelin.com

ZTL and Urban Access Regulations in Europe
w urbanaccess
regulations.eu

RULES OF THE ROAD

ACI
w aci.it

SCOOTER

Rental Motor Bike
w rentalmotorbike.com

CYCLING

Ciclabili Siciliane
w ciclabilisiciliane.com

Ciclofree
w ciclofree.it

Etna Sicily Touring
w etnasicilytouring.com

Sicily Biking Tours
w sicilybikingtours.com

Sicily Cycling
w sicilycycling.com

Social Bike Palermo
w socialbikepalermo.
com

BOATS AND FERRIES

Caronte & Tourist
w carontetourist.it

Liberty Lines
w libertylines.it

SNAV
w snav.it

Tirrenia
w tirrenia.it

Pasqualo
w strombolidamare.it

Sailing Sicily
w sailingsicily.com

WALKING

Outdoor Active
w outdooractive.com

Sicilia Outdoor
w siciliaoutdoor.org

Practical Information

Passports and Visas

For entry requirements, including visas, consult your nearest Italian embassy or check the **Polizia di Stato** website. EU nationals and citizens of the UK, US, Canada, Australia and New Zealand can stay for up to 90 days without a visa, as long as their passport is valid for 6 months beyond the date of entry. A visa is necessary for longer stays and must be obtained in advance from the Italian embassy. All other visitors need valid passports and visas.

Government Advice

Now more than ever, it is important to consult both your and the Italian government's advice before travelling. The **UK Foreign and Commonwealth Office**, the **US Department of State**, the **Australian Department of Foreign Affairs and Trade** and the **Italian Ministero della Salute** offer the latest information on security, health and local regulations.

Customs Information

You can find information on the laws relating to goods and currency taken in or out of Italy on the **ENIT** (Italy's national tourist board) website.

For EU citizens there are no limits on most goods taken in or out of Italy, as long as they are for personal use only. Exceptions include firearms and weapons, endangered species and some types of food and plants. Cash amounts over €10,000 taken into or out of the EU must be declared.

For non-EU citizens, limits vary so check restrictions before departing. Non-EU residents can claim back sales tax (VAT) on purchases over €155 at one store; have your Tax Free forms from the store ready at the airport.

Insurance

We recommend taking out a comprehensive insurance policy covering theft, loss of belongings, medical care, cancellations and delays, and read the small print carefully.

UK citizens are eligible for free emergency medical care in Italy provided they have a valid European Health Insurance Card (**EHIC**) or UK Global Health Insurance Card (**GHIC**). Australia has a reciprocal health care agreement with Italy and citizens should be registered to **Medicare** to receive this benefit. All other nationals should check before travelling.

Health

Italy has a world-class healthcare system. Emergency medical care in Italy is free for all UK, EU and Australian citizens, provided you have an EHIC or GHIC card. If you have a GHIC or EHIC card, be sure to present this as soon as possible. You may have to pay after treatment and reclaim the money later.

For visitors from outside of the UK, EU and Australia, payment of medical expenses is the patient's responsibility, so it's wise to arrange comprehensive medical insurance before travel.

Seek medicinal supplies and advice for minor ailments from pharmacies (farmacia). These are marked with a green cross and sell common drugs, without a prescription. Parafarmacie have a blue or red cross and sell over-the-counter medicines, toiletries and baby formula, and are open on Saturdays. If you run out of your regular medicine, pharmacists may sell replacements, if you have the original packaging. You can find details of the nearest 24-hour service on all pharmacy doors.

Sicily has a network of first aid stations. All tourist resorts operate seasonal emergency treatment centres (guardia medica). Hotels will also be able to suggest English-speaking doctors and dentists if required.

Sicily has no special health issues, but mosquitoes can be bothersome. Spray exposed skin with repellent; if bitten, apply antihistamine cream. When swimming in the sea, it's wise to wear a jellyfish repellent; if stung, remove any stray tenticles with tweezers, soak the skin in hot water and take a pain killer.

During summer, you should wear a hat and sunscreen, stay out of the sun at peak times, and drink plenty of fluids. Tap water is safe to drink but you may prefer the taste of bottled water.

No inoculations are needed for Sicily. For information regarding COVID-19 vaccination requirements, consult government advice.

Smoking, Alcohol and Drugs

Smoking is banned in enclosed public places and the possession of illegal drugs could result in a prison sentence.

Italy has a strict limit of 0.05 per cent BAC (blood alcohol content) for drivers. This means that you cannot drink more than a small beer or a small glass of wine if you plan to drive. For drivers with less than three years' driving experience, and those under 21, the limit is 0.

ID

By law you must carry identification at all times in Italy. A photocopy of your passport photo page (and visa if applicable) should suffice. If you are stopped by the police you may be asked to present the original document within 12 hours.

Personal Security

Sicily is a safe place to visit, but petty crime does take place. Bag-snatching scooter drivers and

pickpockets are known to work busy tourist spots, crowded city centres and public transport, such as ferry ports and train stations. Use common sense, keep belongings close and be alert to your surroundings. If you have anything stolen, report the crime within 24 hours to the nearest police station and take ID with you. If you need to make an insurance claim, get a copy of the crime report *(denuncia)*. Contact your embassy if you have your passport stolen, or in the event of a serious crime.

As a rule, Italians are very accepting of all people, regardless of their race, gender or sexuality. Homosexuality was legalized in 1887 and in 1982 Italy became the third country to recognize the right to legally change your gender. Even so, acceptance is not necessarily a given. Some smaller Sicilian towns and rural areas may be less accepting of LGBTQ+ relationships or sexualities, and overt displays of affection may be received negatively.

Women may receive unwanted and unwelcome attention, especially around tourist areas. If you feel threatened, head straight for the nearest police station.

Italy has two police forces. The **Carabinieri** are the military branch, and the **Polizia di Stato** are the civil branch. Complaints can be filed to either, and both can issue crime or loss reports *(denuncia di furto o smarrimento)*. There are hotlines for the **fire brigade** as well as for the

ambulance. All calls to police and emergency services are free, regardless of the device used to call.

DIRECTORY

PASSPORTS AND VISAS

Polizia di Stato
w poliziadistato.it

GOVERNMENT ADVICE

Australian Department of Foreign Affairs and Trade
w smartraveller.gov.au

Italian Ministero della Salute
w salute.gov.it

UK Foreign and Commonwealth Office
w gov.uk/foreign-travel-advice

US Department of State
w travel.state.gov

CUSTOMS INFORMATION

ENIT
w enit.it

INSURANCE

EHIC
w nhs.uk/ehic

GHIC
w ghic.org.uk

Medicare
w humanservices.gov.au/customer/dhs/medicare

PERSONAL SECURITY

Ambulance
c 118

Carabinieri
c 112
w carabinieri.it

Fire Brigade
c 115

Polizia di Stato
c 113
w poliziadistato.it

Travellers with Specific Requirements

Sicily is ill-equipped for disabled access; however, conditions are improving throughout the island. Ramps, lifts and modified WCs are available in an increasing number of places. Visitors travelling by train can request **RFI** (Italian Railway Network) assistance at the Sala Blu of the Messina train station by visiting the website. **Sicily Accessible Tours** provides information for accessible tours.

Time Zone

Italy operates on Central European Time (CET), one hour ahead of Greenwich Mean Time (GMT), 6 hours ahead of Eastern Standard Time (EST), 9 hours ahead of Pacific Standard Time (PST) and 9 hours behind Australian Eastern Standard Time (AEST). The clock moves forward by one hour during Daylight Saving Time from the last Sunday in March to the last Sunday in October.

Money

Italy is among the 19 European countries that use the euro (€). Most establishments accept major credit and debit, and prepaid currency cards. Contactless payments are widely accepted, but it's always a good idea to carry some cash, as many smaller businesses and markets, especially in more remote areas, still accept cash only. Cash machines are widely found in major

towns, but they are harder to find in remote areas.

Tipping is not expected in restaurants or by taxi drivers, but hotel porters and housekeeping will expect €1 per bag or day.

Electrical Appliances

The electricity supply in Italy is 220 volts. Italian plugs come with two and three round pins, so an adaptor is sometimes necessary – ask for one that will fit both types of plug socket.

Mobile Phones and Wi-Fi

Visitors travelling to Sicily with EU tariffs are able to use their devices without being affected by roaming charges. Users will be charged the same rates for data, SMS and voice calls as they would pay at home.

Your home provider will have roaming options, but check rates carefully before you leave. A cheaper alternative may be to purchase an Italian SIM card, available at all major phone shops. However, you will need to show ID to buy one.

Wi-Fi is generally available in tourist areas, and many cafés and restaurants will usually give you the password for their Wi-Fi on the condition that you make a purchase.

Postal Services

The Italian postal system, **Poste Italiane**, can be slow. If you need to use it, avoid sending registered mail as it tends to accumulate at the collection

point before being sent on. If speed is of the essence for destinations within Italy, use the postal system's courier service, Paccocelere, or for international destinations use a private courier such as **DHL** or **UPS**.

Stamps (francobolli) can be purchased at post offices and tobacconists, and occasionally at shops selling postcards.

Weather

Sicily has a typical Mediterranean climate. The summer heat can be oppressive in inland towns, with cooler temperatures in the mountains. Winters are mild, but snowfall can be copious in mountainous areas. Springtime keeps hotels booked, although it can be blustery. Autumn is prone to downpours.

High season stretches from Easter to July and then from September to October. The majority of the shops and restaurants in the larger cities are closed throughout August because this is when local residents head off to the beaches or mountains to escape the searing heat.

Opening Hours

The days when Sicily's sights shut down for riposo (the long lunch break), or even the entire afternoon, are fast becoming history. The custom of shutting down on Sundays is changing as well.

Most major museums and sights stay open all day, as do an increasing number of supermarkets and international chain stores, with some shops in Palermo staying open around the clock.

Shops, churches and other businesses that still follow tradition will usually open in the morning, close during lunchtime and then reopen in the afternoon. Shops generally close at 8pm. The opening hours for many museums, art galleries and archae-ological sites vary widely, so it is always advisable to check before starting out. Last admission to many attractions is 30 minutes to one hour before closing time.

COVID-19 Increased rates of infection may result in temporary opening hours and/or closures. Always check ahead before visiting museums, attractions and hospitality venues.

Visitor Information

Visitor information offices can be found at all four airports in Sicily, where staff can be helpful in giving suggestions on where to stay; they will also hand out as many free maps as you need.

There are several tourist information points that are dotted around Palermo and Catania, often designated with an "I". In smaller cities tourist information offices are often called Pro Loco.

Local Customs

Italians are relatively relaxed when it comes to etiquette. Strangers usually shake hands, while friends and family greet each other with a kiss on each cheek. But there are some strict rules. In some towns and cities you can be fined for dropping litter, sitting on monument steps, or eating or drinking outside churches, monuments and public buildings. It is an offence to swim or bathe in public fountains.

Illegal traders operate on the streets of all the cities; avoid buying from them as you could be fined by the local police.

Entrance to churches is generally free, but you may be charged a small fee to see a certain area, such as a chapel, cloister or underground ruins. Visiting may be prohibited during Mass. Strict dress codes apply: cover your torso and upper arms, and ensure shorts and skirts cover your knees. Shoes must be worn. Do not talk loudly and don't use cameras or mobile devices without first asking permission.

Language

Italian is the official language, but many people still speak Sicilian dialect. The level of English and other languages can be limited, particularly in rural areas, and locals appreciate visitors' efforts to speak Italian, even if only a few words.

Taxes and Refunds

VAT (called IVA in Italy) is usually 22 per cent, with a reduced rate of 4–10 per cent on some items. Non-EU citizens can claim an IVA rebate subject to certain conditions. It is easier to claim before you buy (you will need to show your passport to the shop assistant and complete a form). If claiming retrospectively, present a customs officer with your purchases and receipts at the airport. Receipts will be stamped and sent back to the vendor to issue a refund.

Accommodation

Sicily has a range of places to stay, from opulent hotels to hostels. Staying in a city centre is convenient, but can often be expensive.

Some resort hotels are closed in the winter. In the summer accommodation is snapped up fast, and prices are ofen inflated. In some cities, such as Palermo and Catania, you will be charged a city tax on top of the price for the room (around €2 per person per night).

Under Italian law, hotels are required to register guests at police headquarters and issue a receipt of payment (ricevuta fifi scale), which you must keep until you leave Italy.

DIRECTORY

TRAVELLERS WITH SPECIFIC REQUIREMENTS

RFI
W rfi.it

Sicily Accessible Tours
W sicilyaccessibletours. com

POSTAL SERVICES

DHL
W dhl.it

Poste Italiane
W poste.it

UPS
W ups.com

Places to Stay

PRICE CATEGORIES
For a standard, double room per night (with breakfast if included), taxes and extra charges.

| € under €100 | €€ €100–€200 | €€€ over €200 |

Luxury Hotels

Eremo della Giubiliana, Ragusa
MAP F5 ▪ Contrada da Giubiliana ▪ 093 2669119 ▪ www.eremodella giubiliana.it ▪ €€
This elegant 15th-century monastic building has rooms and suites converted from friar's cells as well as rustic-chic cottages, ensuring that each of its guests receives attentive service. Rooms, public areas and grounds are authentically restored with wood and iron furnishings, fountains and stone courtyards.

La Moresca Maison de Charme, Marina di Ragusa
MAP F6 ▪ Via Dandolo 63 ▪ 093 21915535 ▪ Closed Dec–Mar ▪ www.la morescahotel.eu ▪ €€
This gorgeous neo-Gothic building, a few metres from the sea, has plush rooms with period art pieces. The buffet breakfast is superb.

Locanda Don Serafino, Ragusa Ibla
MAP F5 ▪ Via XI Febbraio 15 ▪ 093 2220065 ▪ www.locandadonserafino.it ▪ €€
The hotel offers distinct rooms, some of which are carved out of the rocky cliffside to which Ibla clings. There is also a private lido at Marina di Ragusa.

The Ashbee
MAP H3 ▪ Via San Pancrazio 46 ▪ 094 223537 ▪ Closed Feb–Mar ▪ www.theashbeehotel.com ▪ €€€
A short stroll away from Taormina's centre, the Ashbee is a boutique hotel perched on a cliff overlooking the sea. It has 24 guest rooms, a rooftop lounge and lush gardens.

Excelsior Palace Hotel, Taormina
MAP H3 ▪ Via Toselli 8 ▪ 094 223975 ▪ www.excelsiorpalacetaormina.it ▪ €€€
A four-star hotel known for its views of Etna, its gardens and swimming pool are on a ridge overlooking the Bay of Naxos.

Grand Hotel Baia Verde, Catania
MAP G4 ▪ Via Angelo Musco 8/10, Aci Castello ▪ 095 491522 ▪ www.baiaverde.it ▪ €€€
The elegant rooms and suites are all renovated, with living areas and a terrace. They surround the palm-filled pool area and look out to sea.

Grand Hotel Timeo, Taormina
MAP H3 ▪ Via Teatro Greco 59 ▪ 094 26270200 ▪ Closed mid-Jan–mid-Mar ▪ www.belmond.com/hotels/europe/italy/taormina/belmond-grand-hotel-timeo ▪ €€€
This hotel is located in the palm- and bougainvillea-covered hillside below Taormina's ancient Greek theatre. There are 71 rooms decorated in Baroque style. Two restaurants and a bar occupy terraces with great views.

Grand Hotel Villa Igiea, Palermo
MAP L2 ▪ Salita Belmonte 43 ▪ 091 6312111 ▪ www.villa-igiea.com ▪ €€€
Art Nouveau architect Ernesto Basile built this grand villa at the end of the 19th century on the slopes of Monte Pellegrino. Dine on the terraces overlooking the sea.

San Domenico Palace, Taormina
MAP H3 ▪ Piazza San Domenico 5 ▪ 094 2613111 ▪ www.san-domenico-palace.com ▪ €€€
Built as a monastery in the 1400s, San Domenico Palace houses 105 rooms, a fitness room, beauty area, a pool and gym. The hotel offers great views of the bay and Mount Etna.

Terre di Vendicari, Noto
MAP G5 ▪ Contrada Vaddeddi ▪ 346 3593845 ▪ www.terredivendicari.it ▪ €€€
There are only four rooms in these luxuriously renovated farm buildings and they have been decorated in calming white and ochre. Nestle into one of the four-poster beds on the terrace and follow the line of the swimming pool out to the sea on the horizon. The service is attentive.

Historic Hotels

Baglio Spanò, Petrosino, near Marsala

MAP B3 ▪ Contrada Triglia Scaletta ▪ 348 8822095 ▪ www.baglio spano.com ▪ €

A gorgeous country house from the 19th century, Baglio Spanò is set amidst citrus groves. The five traditionally decorated rooms are part of the charm. The hotel has an elevated swimming pool as well.

Hotel L'Ariana, Rinella, Salina

MAP G1 ▪ Via Rotabile 11 ▪ 090 9809075 ▪ www. hotelariana.it ▪ €

This whimsical villa was built onto the rocks above the tiny port of Rinella at the turn of the 20th century and has long been in the same family. Rooms are simple, and the best ones are those on the first floor, which open onto a terrace with great views.

Hotel Relais Modica

MAP G6 ▪ Via Tommaso Campailla 99 ▪ 093 2754451 ▪ www.hotel relaismodica.it ▪ €

This renovated *palazzo* offers lovely views of Modica, a roof garden and family rooms. The service is friendly.

Il Principe Hotel, Catania

MAP G4 ▪ Via Alessi 24 ▪ 095 2500345 ▪ www. ilprincipehotel.com ▪ €

This renovated Baroque-style building is set in the historic heart of Catania. Rooms offer every modern comfort and, for additional luxury, there is a Turkish bath for guests to enjoy.

Atelier sul Mare, Castel di Tusa

MAP E2 ▪ Via Cesare Battisti 4 ▪ 092 1334295 ▪ www.ateliersulmare. com ▪ €€

Of the 41 rooms here, 21 are Art Rooms, with installation pieces created by a modern artist. Each of the rooms has a seafront terrace.

Foresteria Baglio della Luna, Agrigento

MAP D4 ▪ Via S A Guastella 1C, Valle dei Templi ▪ 092 2511061 ▪ www.bagliodellaluna. com ▪ €€

Guests are made to feel at home in this restored 13th-century watchtower and 18th-century villa. The bright central courtyard here leads onto terraces shaded by olive and fruit trees with views out to Agrigento's famed temples *(see pp32–5)*. Rooms on the upper level are furnished with antiques.

Giardino sul Duomo, Ragusa

MAP F5 ▪ Via Dottor Solarino 26/A ▪ 366 5794027 ▪ www.giardino sulduomo.it ▪ €€

This building, set in fine gardens within the town of Ragusa, offers lovely views over Ragusa's cathedral and town centre to the hills and valleys beyond. The 13 large rooms are elegant.

Palazzo Brunaccini, Palermo

MAP L6 ▪ Piazzetta Brunaccini 9 ▪ 091 586904 ▪ www. palazzo brunaccini.it ▪ €€

Located within the city's Jewish quarter, this boutique hotel is a colourful blend of local crafts and Art Deco style. The hotel has a restaurant and a bar.

Hotel Belvedere, Taormina

MAP H3 ▪ Via Bagnoli Croci 79 ▪ 094 223791 ▪ Closed Dec–Feb ▪ www. villabelvedere.it ▪ €€€

This was built as a grand hotel on Taormina's hillside in 1902. Renovations have modernized the guest rooms without losing their original charm (most have good views). The Belvedere is also noted for its pleasant gardens with citrus and palm trees. Lunch is served beside the pool.

Massimo Plaza, Palermo

MAP L4 ▪ Via Maqueda 437 ▪ 091 325657 ▪ www. massimoplazahotel.com ▪ €€€

A renovated *palazzo* with views of the piazza, the Massimo Plaza is located right opposite the opera house, Teatro Massimo. The soundproofed rooms ensure a peaceful stay. However, guests should note that the stairs are steep and there is no lift. On-site parking available.

Villa Athena, Agrigento

MAP D4 ▪ Via Passeggiata Archeologica 33 ▪ 092 2596288 ▪ www.hotel villaathena.it ▪ €€€

A hotel and spa within the Valley of the Temples, Villa Athena offers grand rooms, some with private terraces. It is the only place on the island where you can swim and play tennis with the magnificent temples serving as the backdrop.

Resort Hotels

Approdo di Ulisse, Favignana
MAP A3 ▪ Contrada Calagrande ▪ 092 3921125 ▪ www.aurumhotel.it ▪ €
A tastefully designed resort of whitewashed bungalows and cottages by a series of tiny caves on the west side of the island. Pool, tennis and diving available.

La Dimora di Spartivento, Ragusa
MAP F5 ▪ SS 115, Km 323 ▪ 093 21865377 ▪ www. dimoradispartivento.it ▪ €
In a rural setting with views over the Hyblean plateau and Modica to the sea, this hotel has 23 big rooms equipped with modern amenities, a pool as well as a gym.

Il Piccolo Etna Golf Hotel & Resort, Castiglione di Sicilia
MAP G3 ▪ SS 120, Km 200 ▪ 094 2986384 ▪ www. ilpiccoloetnagolfresort. com ▪ €€
This resort is located on the slopes of Mount Etna. Facilities include an 18-hole golf course, pool, tennis courts, gym as well as a spa.

Kalura Hotel, Cefalù
MAP E2 ▪ Via Vincenzo Cavallaro 13 ▪ 092 1421 354 ▪ Closed mid-Nov–mid-Mar ▪ www.hotel-kalura.com ▪ €€
A Italian seaside hotel with modern rooms, Kalura Hotel offers a range of facilities, including a pool, private beach, billiard tables, tennis courts and mountain bikes. Sailing and horse riding trips can also be organized.

Atlantis Bay, Taormina Mare
MAP H3 ▪ Via Nazionale 161 ▪ 094 2618011 ▪ www. atlantisbay.it ▪ €€€
A hotel with full-service spa and private beach. The pool and terrace for dining are at the water's edge and the rooms have a private terrace with views of the bay.

Capofaro Malvasia & Resort, Salina
MAP G1 ▪ Via Faro 3 ▪ 090 9844330 ▪ www. capofaro.it ▪ €€€
Luxurious rooms with terraces open onto sea or garden views at the Tasca d'Almerita family's five-star resort. Whitewashed buildings are set off by splashes of bougainvillea.

Grand Hotel Minareto, Syracuse
MAP H5 ▪ Via del Faro Massolivieri 26 ▪ 093 1721222 ▪ www.grand hotelminareto.it ▪ €€€
In the natural Plemmirio reserve, this resort has a spa, pools, private beach and two restaurants.

Hotel Villa Sant' Andrea, Taormina
MAP H3 ▪ Via Nazionale 137, Taormina Mare ▪ 094 26271200 ▪ Closed Nov–Apr ▪ www.hotel villa santandrea.com ▪ €€€
The rooms here have terraces with wonderful sea views, and are set in a restored 19th-century villa beneath Monte Tauro.

Raya, Panarea
MAP G1 ▪ Via Pepe e Maria ▪ 090 983013 ▪ Closed Nov–Mar ▪ www.hotelraya.it ▪ €€€
This place is a study in relaxation, where white-washed buildings with large terraces look out to the sea. There is a restaurant right over the water serving fresh fish. Children under 12 are not allowed.

Verdura Resort, Sciacca
MAP C4 ▪ SS 115, Km 131 ▪ 092 5998001 ▪ www. roccofortehotels.com/ hotels-and-resorts/ verdura-resort ▪ €€€
A top-class resort with its own stretch of coastline, an 18-hole championship golf course and a spa. Its location makes it ideal for trips to Agrigento and Selinunte.

Comfortable Hotels

Albergo Maccotta, Trapani
MAP B2 ▪ Via Degli Argentieri 4 ▪ 092 328418 ▪ www.albergomaccotta. it ▪ €
The Albergo Maccotta has an excellent location in Trapani's historic centre. Rooms are simple and clean.

Hotel Aegusa, Favignana
MAP A3 ▪ Via Garibaldi 11 ▪ 092 3921739 ▪ www. aegusa hotel.it ▪ €
Book a stay here for its modern rooms, a terrace and a small garden restaurant, all tucked away in Favignana town.

Hotel Il Barocco, Ragusa Ibla
MAP F5 ▪ Via Santa Maria La Nuova 1 ▪ 093 2663105 ▪ www.ilbarocco.it ▪ €
At this centrally located hotel, the staff are helpful, parking is available and there is a breakfast room on site. The hotel is a great base for exploring southeast Sicily.

Hotel Miramare, Selinunte

MAP B4 ▪ Via Pigafetta 2 ▪ 092 446666 ▪ www. hotelmiramareselinunte. it ▪ €

The Miramare hotel overlooks the Mediterranean sea, and has a breathtaking view of the nearby Acropolis of Selinunte. It has a private beach, piano bar and pizzeria. It also offers Wi-Fi and parking.

Katane Palace Hotel, Catania

MAP G4 ▪ Via C. Finocchiaro Aprile 110 ▪ 095 7470702 ▪ www. katanepalace.it ▪ €

This modern hotel with spacious rooms in a renovated *palazzo* is just steps away from one of the city's daily markets and the chic Via Etnea. It has helpful staff, a bar as well as an on-site restaurant. Parking is available, but book in advance.

Relais Antiche Saline, Paceco

MAP B2 ▪ Via Verdi, Località Nubia ▪ 092 386 8042 ▪ www.relais antiche saline.it/site/ hotel ▪ €

Set in a renovated historic building with spacious rooms offering views over the Egadi Islands and the saltpans of Trapani's coast, this hotel has a pool area, an outdoor spa with a Finnish sauna and a good restaurant. Transport to Trapani upon request.

Centrale Palace Hotel, Palermo

MAP D2 ▪ Via Vittorio Emanuele 327 ▪ 093 2959908 ▪ www.euro starhotels.ie ▪ €€

This hotel occupies an elegant, restored *palazzo*

with luxurious marble-clad public areas. Guests can enjoy romantic dinners and splendid views on the roof terrace.

Hotel Elios, Taormina

MAP H3 ▪ Via Bagnoli Croci 98 ▪ 094 223431 ▪ www.elioshotel.com ▪ €€

A family-run hotel below the Teatro Antico, Hotel Elios features comfortable and spacious rooms, and almost all have sea views. It has lounge chairs to relax on the rooftop.

Hotel Gutkowski, Syracuse

MAP H5 ▪ Lungomare di Levenate 26 ▪ 093 1465861 ▪ www.gut hotel.it ▪ €€

In summer, breakfast is served on the terrace at this hotel on the Ortygia seafront. Gutkowski has its own restaurant as well.

Hotel Pomara, San Michele di Ganzaria

MAP F4 ▪ Via Vittorio Veneto 84 ▪ 093 3978142 ▪ www.hotelpomara.com ▪ €€

The Pomara is one of the most comfortable inland options. The location is rustic with views of the rolling hills. It has a great restaurant, and is convenient for visiting sites such as Enna, Piazza Armerina, Morgantina as well as Caltagirone.

Hotel Posta, Palermo

MAP D2 ▪ Via Antonio Gagini 77 ▪ 091 587338 ▪ www.hotelposta palermo.it ▪ €€

This three-star hotel is an excellent bargain option in Palermo. The rooms

are spacious and clean, the public areas have TVs, and parking is available. The hotel is near the church of San Domenico.

La Sirena, Filicudi

MAP H3 ▪ Via Pecorini a Mare ▪ 090 9889997 ▪ Closed Oct–May ▪ www.pensionela sirena.it ▪ €€

A laidback and intimate *pensione* on the remote island of Filicudi. La Sirena has four airy rooms with balconies overlooking the harbour, which is always full of bobbing fishing boats. There's a restaurant, bar and lido, plus a fantastic takeaway sushi bar next door. Breakfast and discounts for lunch are included.

Agriturismo and B&Bs

La Zagara, Furci Siculo

MAP H2 ▪ Via Manzoni 5 ▪ 338 2178989 ▪ www. lazagarabeb.it ▪ €

Located in a village near Taormina, just steps from the beach, the five rooms here have private bathrooms and balconies with sea views.

Sotto i Pini, Zafferana Etnea

MAP G3 ▪ Via A Diaz 208, Pisano ▪ 095 956696 ▪ www.sottoipini.it ▪ €

A charming and historic villa set in its own vineyards, olive groves and orchards, offering views of Mount Etna and the sea. Breakfast features organic, seasonal, local produce, much of it home-grown.

For a key to hotel price categories see p142

Torre di Renda, Enna
MAP E4 ▪ Piazza Armerina ▪ 093 5680208 ▪ www.torrerenda.it ▪ €
This is a rustic *agriturismo* in the hills around Piazza Armerina. Guided bicycle tours of town are available. There is a swimming pool and restaurant on site.

Baglio Fontanasalsa, Trapani
MAP B2 ▪ Via Cusenza 78 ▪ 092 3591001 ▪ www.fontanasalsa.it ▪ €€
This *agriturismo* is a working olive farm on an 18th-century property, with rustic rooms, play areas for children and citrus orchards.

BB 22, Palermo
MAP D2 ▪ Via Pantelleria 22 (junction Largo Cavalieri di Malta) ▪ 091 326214 ▪ www.bb22.it ▪ €€
Housed in a restored *palazzo*, this B&B has rooms with feather tassels on the gilt bureau, hot-pink terry-covered bath furniture as well as armoires with lovely Eastern motifs.

Locanda COS, Vittoria
MAP F5 ▪ SP3, Km 14, 300 ▪ 390 932876145 ▪ www.cosvittoria.it ▪ €€
Restored farmhouses on the grounds of the COS winery have been turned into apartments with high domed ceilings and balconies. Enjoy traditional meals and the lovely pool area. Winery tours available on request.

Mandranova, Palma di Montechiaro
MAP D5 ▪ SS 115, Km 217 ▪ 393 9862169 ▪ www.mandranova.com ▪ €€
Producing award-winning olive oil, Mandranova is

nestled between the sea and the coastline, where old farmhouses have been converted into rooms and suites. On-site facilities include a swimming pool, reading room, billiards hall and cooking courses.

Masseria Susafa, Polizzi Generosa
MAP E3 ▪ Contrada Susafa ▪ 338 9608713 ▪ www.susafa.com ▪ €€
This converted farmhouse in the Madonie mountains has a rustic glamour. The rooms accommodate two to six people. There is an on-site restaurant as well.

Talia, Modica
MAP G6 ▪ Via Exaudinos 1/9 ▪ 093 2752075 ▪ www.casatalia.it ▪ €€
Stone houses in Modica's ancient ghetto have been carefully renovated and linked via original terraced gardens and stone staircases. The rooms are minimally decorated with Sicilian materials.

Self-Catering and Villas

Agrituristica Villa Levante, Castelbuono
MAP E3 ▪ Via Isnello ▪ 335 6394574 ▪ www.villalevante.it ▪ €
Four restored self-catering apartments are set in a 19th-century castle with gardens and a farm producing olive oil. There are marked trails for walks, hikes and mountain biking.

Apartments Casa Giudecca, Cefalù
MAP E2 ▪ Via Candeloro 105 ▪ 092 1922339 ▪ www.bookingcefalu.com ▪ €
Apartments for rent to the east of Cefalù built on a

cliffside, with balconies overlooking the sea, and steps down the cliffs.

B&B Enza Marturano, Lipari
MAP G1 ▪ Via Maurolico 35 ▪ 368 3224997 ▪ No credit cards ▪ www.enzamarturano.it ▪ €€
In the centre of Lipari, not far from the Marina Corta, this place features four bright private rooms with cooking facilities. Rooms are grouped around a communal sitting room, kitchen and terrace.

Bagolaro
MAP G3 ▪ Viagrande ▪ 075 5057865 ▪ www.homeinitaly.com ▪ €€€
Located in Viagrande, this elegant, 17th-century stone villa has been expanded with contemporary elements such as a sleek glasshouse overlooking the swimming pool and manicured grounds.

Pensione and Monasteries

Il Giardino del Barocco, Noto
MAP G5 ▪ Via Aurispa Giovanni 77 ▪ 093 1573919 ▪ www.ilgiardinodelbarocco.it ▪ €
This small *pensione* is set in a historic palace with a courtyard garden in the city centre.

La Giara, Nicolosi
MAP G3 ▪ Viale della Regione 12 A ▪ 095 7919022 ▪ www.giara.it ▪ €
Spacious rooms and colourful decor make this place an appealing base for exploring Mount Etna. There is a large terrace with views up to the volcano.

Monastero di San Benedetto, Modica

MAP G6 ▪ Via S Benedetto da Norcia 101 ▪ 093 2941033 ▪ No credit cards ▪ €

A few minutes' walk from the station, this monastery, founded in 1892, has single, non-airconditioned bedrooms as well as a refectory. It is mainly for religious retreats.

Pensione Tranchina, Scopello

MAP C2 ▪ Via A Diaz 7 ▪ 092 4541099 ▪ www.pensionetranchina.com ▪ €

A charming *pensione* in a tiny fishing village, with decorated rooms that have iron or wooden bedsteads; several have a sea view. The owners cook excellent Sicilian cuisine, mainly using fresh seafood and garden vegetables.

SoleLuna della Solidarietà, Palermo

MAP D2 ▪ Via Vincenzo Riolo 7 ▪ 091 581671 ▪ www.solelunabedand breakfast.org ▪ €

Each room here has its own private, though not en-suite, bathroom. The owner donates 5 per cent of her proceeds to a local youth group; she also offers tours of Palermo.

Albergo Domus Mariae, Ortygia

MAP H5 ▪ Via Vittorio Veneto 76 ▪ 093 124854 ▪ www.domusmariae benessere.com ▪ €€

The Ursuline sisters run a modern hotel in a restored 19th-century *palazzo* on Ortygia. All rooms have air conditioning; some have a sea view. Book in advance.

Pocho, San Vito lo Capo

MAP B2 ▪ Localita Isulidda ▪ 092 3972525 ▪ www.hotel-pocho.it ▪ €€

A small *pensione* with comfortable rooms, some decorated with items from a traditional Sicilian puppet theatre. There is a terrace restaurant, sea views and a beach nearby.

Campsites and Hostels

Baia dei Coralli, Palermo

MAP D2 ▪ Via Plauto 27, Sferracavallo ▪ 091 7785080 ▪ www.aighostels.it ▪ €

Just a few steps from the beach in a seaside resort, this hostel sleeps 76 in double or four-bed rooms. It's a short bus ride from Palermo.

Camping Baia Unci, Lipari

MAP G1 ▪ Via Marina Garibaldi 3/7, Canneto ▪ 090 9811909 ▪ www.campingbaiaunci.it ▪ €

Set on a beautiful bay on the island of Lipari, this well-shaded campsite takes tents, campervans and caravans. Also available are fully furnished, air-conditioned bunga-lows for 2–6 people.

Camping Costa Ponente, Cefalù

MAP E2 ▪ Contrada Ogliastrillo SS 113 ▪ 092 1420085 ▪ Closed Nov–Mar ▪ No credit cards ▪ camping-costaponente. com ▪ €

A three-star campsite with spots for tents and caravans, a swimming pool, tennis courts and access to the beach below.

Its facilities include a bar, small market and self-service restaurant.

Camping La Focetta Sicula, Sant'Alessio Siculo

MAP H3 ▪ Contrada Siena 40 ▪ 094 2751657 ▪ www. lafocetta.it ▪ €

Located right by the sea, this campsite has 85 beds in furnished bungalows and mobile homes with air conditioning, heating and with a shaded terrace or veranda.

Il Forte Camping Village, Marzamemi

MAP G6 ▪ Contrada Spinazza ▪ 093 1841011 ▪ www.ilfortevillage.it ▪ €

This camping village with bungalows and parking is located near a sandy beach. Facilities include public telephones, a bar, restaurant and market, as well as diving, boat, bike and scooter hire.

Ostello Degli Elefanti, Catania

MAP G4 ▪ Via Etnea 28 ▪ 095 2265691 ▪ www. ostellodeglielefanti.it ▪ €

Set in a 17th-century *palazzo*, just steps from Piazza Duomo, this hostel offers dorms and private rooms, a reading room, kitchen and a rooftop terrace with views of Mount Etna.

Taormina's Odyssey, Taormina

MAP H3 ▪ Via Paterno di Biscari 13 ▪ 094 224533 ▪ www.taorminaodyssey. com ▪ €

There's a very friendly atmosphere at this hostel in the residential part of Taormina, a short walk from the centre. Private rooms or dormitory.

For a key to hotel price categories see p142

General Index

Acknowledgments

Author

Elaine Trigiani is a Sicilian-American art historian living in Italy since 1998. A certified olive-oil taster, she designs and leads tavel programmes, as well as running cooking classes in Sicily, Tuscany and the US.

Additional contributor
Conchita Vecchio

Publishing Director Georgina Dee

Publisher Vivien Antwi

Design Director Phil Ormerod

Editorial Ankita Awasthi Tröger, Rebecca Flynn, Rachel Fox, Maresa Manara, Scarlett O'Hara, Sally Schafer, Farah Sheikh

Cover Design Maxine Pedliham, Vinita Venugopal

Design Marisa Renzullo, Vinita Venugopal

Picture Research Subhadeep Biswas, Taiyaba Khatoon, Sumita Khatwani, Ellen Root

Cartography James McDonald, Casper Morris, Animesh Pathak, John Plumer

DTP Jason Little

Production Igrain Roberts

Factchecker Toni DeBella

Proofreader Kathryn Glendenning

Indexer Helen Peters

Illustrator Chris Orr & Associates chrisorr.com

First edition created by Sargasso Media Ltd, London

Revisions Parnika Bagla, Sumita Khatwani, Shikha Kulkarni, Arushi Mathur, Meghna, Bandana Paul, Beverly Smart, Priyanka Thakur, Stuti Tiwari, Tanveer Zaidi

Commissioned Photography Amanda Heywood, Demetrio Carrasco, Nigel Hicks, Bridget Williams

Picture Credits

The publisher would like to thank the following for their kind permission to reproduce their photographs:
Key: a-above; b-below/bottom; c-centre; f-far; l-left; r-right; t-top

123RF.com: Giuseppe Anello 54clb, 75tr; Yury Dmitrienko 99cr; lsantilli 81tr.

Le 4 Stagioni, Menfi: 105bc.

4Corners: Antonino Bartuccio 14br, 16cl, 17tl, 28-9c, 36-7t, 80bl, 87cla; Gabriele Croppi 121b; Giorgio Filippini 17crb; Johanna Huber 25crb; SIME / Paolo Giocoso 13tl, 13c, 16br, 22-3; Alessandro Saffo 4cra, 26t, 48tl, 84b, 113tl; Sebastiano Scattolin 24-5c.

Accursio: 79cr.

Alamy Stock Photo: Arcaid Images 45tr; Diego Barucco 128cla; Bon Appetit 122tl; Dennis Cox 35br; Cultura Creative 3tr, 132-3; Stephen Emerson 18-19c; EmmePi Travel 71tr; Giulio Ercolani 7tr, 125t; Findlay 19br; funkyfood London / Paul Williams 15tr, 19tl, 20-21b; Roger Goodwin 20cla; Hemis 31bl; imageBROKER 14-15c, 69tr, 96tl; Ingolf Pompe 86 72b; Ivy Close Image 120clb; Yadid Levy 50t; LOOK Die Bildagentur der Fotografen GmbH 97clb; Marshall Ikonography 120ca; mauritius images GmbH / ClickAlps 21tl, Visual&Written SL / WPICS / HAL BERAL 21crb; Angus McComiskey 33tl; Sandro Messina 114tl; Francesco Palermo 50bl; Photo 12 57tr; Photolocate 6c; Massimo Piacentino 28bl, 125crb; Domenico Piccione 14cl, Realy Easy Star / Toni Spagone 28crb, 29cr, 81cl, 82t; REDA &CO srl 34crb, 34bl, 61cra; Rolf Richardson 10tr; Rolf Nussbaumer Photography / Stefan Huwiler 10crb; Romas_ph 92cra; Roberto Lo Savio 2tl, 8-9; Peter Scholey 35t, 36bl, 51c; Neil Setchfield 29tl; Ivan Vdovin 2tr, 4crb, 40-41; Martyn Vickery 83clb; WaterFrame 64b; Westend61 GmbH 54tr; Jan Wlodarczyk 3tl, 24br, 88-9, 106-7; Michal Zieba 72tr.

The Antonio Pasqualino International Puppet Museum: 68br.

AWL Images: Neil Farrin 11tr; Hemis 65cla, 109cl; Katja Kreder 4t, 60t, 100cl; Sabine Lubenow 86crb; Ken Scicluna 33crb; Maurizio Rellini 1; Marco Simoni 16-17c, 46bl, 100-101bc.

Cantavespri: 73cl.

Cantine Pellegrino, Marsala: 104tl.

Capitolo Primo: 123crb.

La Capinera: 115cra.

Le Colonne, Taormina: 82cb.

La Coppola Storta: 95c.

La Darsena da Iannuzzo, Syracuse: 131cra.

Depositphotos Inc: agiampiccolo 124tl; boggy22 30-31c; elisalocci 126cl; giuliaisabella 68tl; siculodoc 30cl.

Dreamstime Inc: Al1962 76tl, 81bc; Ivan Vander Biesen 47tr; Delstudio 113cr; Dianaphotography 4cla; Yury Dmitrienko 102t; Sabrina Dvihally 118tl; Ebastard129 85clb, 112b, Ellesi 103bl, Emicristea 32-3b, Eugenia Struk 85tr; Marzia Giacobbe 76bl; William Giannelli 83tr; Yulia Grigoryeva 122br; Kityyaya 48b; Vladimir Korostyshevskiy 94cla; Lachris77 30crb, 73br, 114br; Lev Levin 38cl; Elisa Locci 24cla; Lorenzograph 77cl; Anna Lurye 6b, 10b, 18cl, 126br, 130b; Mahroch 11crb; Marcorubino 49crb; Stanisa Martinovic 45cl; Marzolino 52-3bc, 84tr; Mattiaath 65br; Martin Molcan 62-3; Nanisimova 110-11t; Pavlinec 44tr, 53cla; Ariadna De Raadt 105cl; Ralligeller 44b; Andrea G. Ricordi 103cr; Jozef Sedmak 12clb, 13bl, 91br; Denise Serra 117ca; Siculodoc 69cl; Alessandro Antonio Storniolo 55tr; Thevirex 87br; Travelling-light 123ca;

Raluca Tudor 77tr; Tupungato 116ca; Denisa Vlaicu 109cra; Vvoevale 19cr, 75cl, 77bl; Andreas Zerndl 46t.

Ristorante Duomo: 79bc.

Getty Images: Stefano Bianchetti 42b, 56t; Culture Club 53tr; De Agostini Picture Library 39crb, / Archivio J. Lange 38tr, / G. Cappellani 39b, / G. Cigolini 43cl, / G. Dagli Orti 4clb, 37cb, 42tc, 43br, / G. Nimatallah 90tl; LatitudeStock - Mel Longhurst 31tl; Maremagnum 59tr; Fabio Montalto 78b; Vittoriano Rastelli 57bl; Roberto Soncin Gerometta 74bl; Slow Images 4cl, 11cra, 108tl; UniversalImagesGroup 55bl.

Internazionale delle Marionette Pasqualino, Palermo: Dorling Kindersley / Demetrio Carrasco 51tr.

iStockphoto.com: alxpin 12-13c; Brzozowska 4b, 98ca; eddygaleotti 91tr; eZeePics Studio 76c; helovi 52tl; Krivinis 118bc; kruwt 127cl; lucamato 38c; master2 60bl, 94b; Rimbalzino 59b; Rolf_52 95tr; RolfSt 11bl; ROMAOSLO 92-3b; SalvoV 11tl; Satephoto 58cl; vladj55 119cla; VvoeVale 117br.

I Luoghi del Lavoro Contadino, Buscemi: 129tr.

Majore, Chiaramonte Gulfi: 78cla.

Museo Geologico Gemellaro, Palermo: 66cla.

Opera dei Pupi di Enzo Mancuso, Palermo: 71b.

Pepe Rosa, Bronte: 115cb.

Regione Siciliana -Dipartimento dei Beni Culturali e dell'Identità Siciliana: 26br, 27tr, 27cl, 27br.

Robert Harding Picture Library: Sabine Lubenow 11clb, 110bl, 111cl; Matthew Williams-Ellis 64tl.

SuperStock: Art Archive 56crb; Cubo Images 74cla; Cubo Images / Giuseppe Greco 128br; DeAgostini 37tl; age fotostock / Mike Randolph 80tr; imageBROKER 72tl, / Martin Moxter 70clb; Melvyn Longhurst 101tl; Marka 67cla; Travel Library Limited 32cla.

Cover
Front and spine: **AWL Images:** Maurizio Rellini.

Back: **AWL Images:** Maurizio Rellini b; **Getty Images:** EyeEm / Monica Buzzone tr; **iStockphoto.com:** alexsalcedo tl, e55evu cla, unknown1861 crb.

Pull Out Map Cover
AWL Images: Maurizio Rellini.

All other images © Dorling Kindersley

Penguin Random House

First edition 2003

First published in Great Britain by Dorling Kindersley Limited, DK, One Embassy Gardens, 8 Viaduct Gardens, London SW11 7BW, UK

The authorised representative in the EEA is Dorling Kindersley Verlag GmbH. Arnulfstr. 124, 80636 Munich, Germany

Published in the United States by DK US, 1450 Broadway, Suite 801, New York, NY 10018, USA

Copyright © 2003, 2022 Dorling Kindersley Limited

A Penguin Random House Company

21 22 23 24 10 9 8 7 6 5 4 3 2 1

Reprinted with revisions 2005, 2007, 2009, 2011, 2013, 2015, 2018, 2020, 2022

All rights reserved.

No part of this publication may be reproduced, stored in or introduced into a retrieval system, or transmitted in any form, or by any means (electronic, mechanical, photocopying, recording or otherwise) without the prior written permission of the copyright owner.

The publisher cannot accept responsibility for any consequences arising from the use of this book, nor for any material on third party websites, and cannot guarantee that any website address in this book will be a suitable source of travel information.

A CIP catalogue record is available from the British Library.

A catalogue record for this book is available from the Library of Congress.

ISSN 1479-344X

ISBN 978-02415-6599-5

Printed and bound in China

www.dk.com

As a guide to abbreviations in visitor information blocks: **Adm** = admission charge; **D** = dinner.

MIX

er from
ble sources

C018179

n Forest
ertified
n DK's
able future.
to
:pledge

Dk Eyewitness Top 10
06/06/2022

DISCARD

Phrase Book

In an Emergency

Help!	**Aiuto!**	*eye-yoo-toh!*
Stop!	**Fermo!**	*fair-moh!*
Call a doctor	**Chiama un medico**	*kee-ah-mah oon meh-dee-koh*
Call an ambulance	**Chiama un' ambulanza**	*kee-ah-mah oon am-boo-lan-tsa*
Call the police	**Chiama la polizia**	*kee-ah-mah lah pol-ee-tsee-ah*
Call the fire brigade	**Chiama i pompier**	*kee-ah-mah ee pom-pee-air-ee*

Communication Essentials

Yes/No	**Sì/No**	*see/noh*
Please	**Per favore**	*pair fah-vor-eh*
Thank you	**Grazie**	*grah-tsee-eh*
Excuse me	**Mi scusi**	*mee skoo-zee*
Hello/good day	**Buon giorno**	*bwon jor-noh*
Goodbye	**Arrivederci**	*ah-ree-veh-dair-chee*
Good evening	**Buona sera**	*bwon-ah sair-ah*
What?	**Cosa?**	*koh-sah?*
When?	**Quando?**	*kwan-doh?*
Why?	**Perchè?**	*pair-keh?*
Where?	**Dove?**	*doh-veh?*

Useful Phrases

How are you?	**Come sta?**	*koh-meh stah?*
Very well, thank you	**Molto bene, grazie**	*moll-toh beh-neh grah-tsee-eh*
Pleased to meet you	**Piacere di conoscerla**	*pee-ah-chair-eh dee-koh-noh-shair-lah*
Where is/are …?	**Dov'è/ Dove sono …?**	*dov-eh/doveh soh-noh?*
How do I get to …?	**Come faccio per arrivare a …?**	*koh-meh fah-choh pair arri-var-eh ah …?*
Do you speak English?	**Parla inglese?**	*par-lah een-gleh-zeh?*
I don't understand	**Non capisco**	*non ka-pee-skoh*
I'm sorry	**Mi dispiace**	*mee dee-spee-ah-cheh*

Shopping

How much does this cost?	**Quant'è, per favore?**	*kwan-teh pair fah-vor-eh?*
I would like …	**Vorrei …**	*vor-ray …*
Do you have …?	**Avete …?**	*ah-veh-teh …?*
Do you take credit cards?	**Accettate carte di credito?**	*ah-chet-tah-teh kar-teh dee creh-dee-toh?*
What time do you open /close?	**A che ora apre/ chiude?**	*ah keh or-ah-preh/kee-oo-deh?*
this one	**questo**	*kweh-stoh*
that one	**quello**	*kwell-oh*
expensive	**caro**	*kar-oh*
cheap	**un buon prezzo**	*oon bwon pret-soh*
size (clothes)	**la taglia**	*lah tah-lee-ah*
size (shoes)	**il numero**	*eel noo-mair-oh*
white	**bianco**	*bee-ang-koh*
black	**nero**	*neh-roh*
red	**rosso**	*ross-oh*
yellow	**giallo**	*jal-loh*
green	**verde**	*vair-deh*
blue	**blu**	*bloo*

Types of Shop

bakery	**il forno /il panificio**	*eel forn-oh /eel pan-ee-fee-choh*
bank	**la banca**	*lah bang-kah*
bookshop	**la libreria**	*lah lee-breh-ree-ah*
cake shop	**la pasticceria**	*lah pas-tee-chair-ee-ah*
chemist	**la farmacia**	*lah far-mah-chee-ah*
delicatessen	**la salumeria**	*lah sah-loo-meh-ree-ah*
department store	**il grande magazzino**	*eel gran-deh mag-gad-zee-noh*
grocery	**alimentari**	*ah-lee-men-tah-ree*
hairdresser	**il parrucchiere**	*eel par-oo-kee-air-eh*
ice-cream parlour	**la gelateria**	*lah jel-lah-tair-ee-ah*
market	**il mercato**	*eel mair-kah-toh*
newsstand	**l'edicola**	*leh-dee-koh-lah*
post office	**l'ufficio postale**	*loo-fee-choh pos-tah-leh*
supermarket	**il supermercato**	*eel su-pair-mair-kah-toh*
tobacconist	**il tabaccaio**	*eel tah-bak-eye-oh*
travel agency	**l'agenzia di viaggi**	*lah-jen-tsee-ah dee vee-ad-jee*

Sightseeing

art gallery	**la pinacoteca**	*lah peena-koh-teh-kah*
bus stop	**la fermata dell'autobus**	*lah fair-mah-tah dell ow-toh-booss*
church	**la chiesa la basilica**	*lah kee-eh-zah lah bah-seel-i-kah*
closed for holidays	**chiuso per le ferie**	*kee-oo-zoh pair leh fair-ee-eh*
garden	**il giardino**	*eel jar-dee-no*
museum	**il museo**	*eel moo-zeh-oh*
railway station	**la stazione**	*lah stah-tsee-oh-neh*
tourist information	**l'ufficio di turismo**	*loo-fee-choh dee too-ree-smoh*

Staying in a Hotel

Do you have any vacant rooms?	**Avete camere libere?**	*ah-veh-teh kah-mair-eh lee-bair-eh?*
double room	**una camera doppia**	*oona kah-mair-ah doh-pee-ah*
with double bed	**con letto matrimoniale**	*kon let-toh mah-tree-moh-nee-ah-leh*
twin room	**una camera con due letti**	*oona kah-mair-ah kon doo-eh let-tee*
single room	**una camera singola**	*oona kah-mair-ah sing-goh-lah*
room with a bath/shower	**una camera con bagno, con doccia**	*oona kah-mair-ah kon ban-yoh, kon dot-chah*
I have a reservation	**Ho fatto una prenotazione**	*oh fat-toh oona preh-noh-tah-tsee-oh-neh*

Eating Out

Have you got a table for …?	**Avete una tavola per …?**	ah-veh-teh oona tah-voh-lah pair …?
I'd like to reserve a table	**Vorrei riservare una tavola**	vor-ray ree-sair-vah-reh oona tah-voh-lah
breakfast	**la colazione**	lah koh-lah-tsee-oh-neh
lunch	**il pranzo**	eel pran-tsoh
dinner	**la cena**	lah cheh-nah
the bill	**il conto**	eel kon-toh
waitress	**cameriera**	kah-mair-ee-air-ah
waiter	**cameriere**	kah-mair-ee-air-eh
fixed price menu	**il menù a prezzo fisso**	eel meh-noo ah pret-soh fee-soh
dish of the day	**il piatto del giorno**	eel pee-ah-toh dell jor-no
starter	**antipasto**	an-tee-pass-toh
first course	**il primo**	eel pree-moh
main course	**il secondo**	eel seh-kon-doh
vegetables	**contorni**	eel kon-tor-noh
dessert	**il dolce**	eel doll-cheh
cover charge	**il coperto**	eel koh-pair-toh
wine list	**la lista dei vino**	lah lee-stah day veen-oh
glass	**il bicchiere**	eel bee-kee-air-eh
bottle	**la bottiglia**	lah bot-teel-yah
knife	**il coltello**	eel kol-tell-oh
fork	**la forchetta**	lah for-ket-tah
spoon	**il cucchiaio**	eel koo-kee-eye-oh

Menu Decoder

l'acqua minerale	lah-kwah mee-nair-ah-leh	mineral water
gassata/ naturale	gah-zah-tah/ nah-too-rah-leh	fizzy/still
l'agnello	lah-niell-oh	lamb
l'aglio	lal-ee-oh	garlic
al forno	al for-noh	baked
alla griglia	ah-lah greel-yah	grilled
la birra	lah beer-rah	beer
la bistecca	lah bee-stek-kah	steak
il burro	eel boor-oh	butter
il caffè	eel kah-feh	coffee
la carne	la kar-neh	meat
carne di maiale	kar-neh dee mah-yah-leh	pork
la cipolla	la chip-oh-lah	onion
i fagioli	ee fah-joh-lee	beans
il formaggio	eel for-mad-joh	cheese
il fritto misto	eel free-toh mees-toh	mixed fried dish
la frutta	la froot-tah	fruit
frutti di mare	froo-tee dee mah-reh	seafood
i funghi	ee foon-ghee	mushrooms
i gamberi	ee gam-bair-ee	prawns
il gelato	eel jel-ah-toh	ice cream
l'insalata	leen-sah-lah-tah	salad
il latte	eel laht-teh	milk
il manzo	eel man-tsoh	beef
l'olio	loh-lee-oh	oil
il pane	eel pah-neh	bread
le patate	leh pah-tah-teh	potatoes
le patatine fritte	leh pah-tah-teen-eh free-teh	chips
il pepe	eel peh-peh	pepper
il pesce	eel pesh-eh	fish
il pollo	eel poll-oh	chicken
il pomodoro	eel poh-moh-dor-oh	tomato
il prosciutto	eel pro-shoo-toh	ham
il riso	eel ree-zoh	rice
il sale	eel sah-leh	salt
la salsiccia	lah sal-see-chah	sausage
il succo d'arancia/ di limone	eel soo-koh dah-ran-chah/ dee lee-moh-neh	orange/lemon juice
il tè	eel teh	tea
la torta	lah tor-tah	cake/tart
l'uovo	loo-oh-voh	egg
vino bianco	vee-noh bee-ang-koh	white wine
vino rosso	vee-noh ross-oh	red wine
le vongole	leh von-goh-leh	clams
lo zucchero	loh zoo-kair-oh	sugar
la zuppa	lah tsoo-pah	soup

Numbers

1	**uno**	oo-noh
2	**due**	doo-eh
3	**tre**	treh
4	**quattro**	kwat-roh
5	**cinque**	ching-kweh
6	**sei**	say-ee
7	**sette**	set-teh
8	**otto**	ot-toh
9	**nove**	noh-veh
10	**dieci**	dee-eh-chee
11	**undici**	oon-dee-chee
12	**dodici**	doh-dee-chee
13	**tredici**	tray-dee-chee
14	**quattordici**	kwat-tor-dee-chee
15	**quindici**	kwin-dee-chee
16	**sedici**	say-dee-chee
17	**diciassette**	dee-chah-set-teh
18	**diciotto**	dee-chot-toh
19	**diciannove**	dee-chah-noh-veh
20	**venti**	ven-tee
30	**trenta**	tren-tah
40	**quaranta**	kwah-ran-tah
50	**cinquanta**	ching-kwan-tah
60	**sessanta**	sess-an-tah
70	**settanta**	set-tan-tah
80	**ottanta**	ot-tan-tah
90	**novanta**	noh-van-tah
100	**cento**	chen-toh
1,000	**mille**	mee-leh
2,000	**duemila**	doo-eh mee-lah
1,000,000	**un milione**	oon meel-yoh-neh

Time

one minute	**un minuto**	oon mee-noo-toh
one hour	**un'ora**	oon or-ah
a day	**un giorno**	oon jor-noh
Monday	**lunedì**	loo-neh-dee
Tuesday	**martedì**	mar-teh-dee
Wednesday	**mercoledì**	mair-koh-leh-dee
Thursday	**giovedì**	joh-veh-dee
Friday	**venerdì**	ven-air-dee
Saturday	**sabato**	sah-bah-toh
Sunday	**domenica**	doh-meh-nee-kah